Annuals
FOR

DUMMIES®

PORTABLE EDITION

by Bill Marken
& the Editors of The National
Gardening Association

WILEY

Wiley Publishing, Inc.

Annuals For Dummies,® Portable Edition

Published by
Wiley Publishing, Inc.
111 River St.
Hoboken, NJ 07030-5774
www.wiley.com

Copyright © 2006 by Wiley Publishing, Inc., Indianapolis, Indiana

Published by Wiley Publishing, Inc., Indianapolis, Indiana

For general information on our other products and services, please contact our Customer Care Department within the U.S. at 800-762-2974, outside the U.S. at 317-572-3993, or fax 317-572-4002.

For technical support, please visit www.wiley.com/techsupport.

Wiley also publishes its books in a variety of electronic formats. Some content that appears in print may not be available in electronic books.

Library of Congress Control Number: 2006922229

ISBN-13: 978-0-470-04369-1

ISBN-10: 0-470-04369-5

Manufactured in the United States of America

10 9 8 7 6 5 4 3 2 1

1B/QR/QT/QW/IN

WILEY

About the Authors

Bill Marken is an editor and writer who lives in the San Francisco Bay Area. Having developed an early interest in gardening by working at nurseries while going to school, Bill may have been the only English major at the University of California at Berkeley who knew what U.C. soil mix was. Bill is currently serving as editor in chief of *Garden Design* magazine. He is a past winner of the American Horticultural Society's Horticultural Communication Award.

The National Gardening Association is the largest member-based, nonprofit organization of home gardeners in the United States. Founded in 1972 (as "Gardens for All") to spearhead the community garden movement, today's National Gardening Association is best known for its bimonthly magazine, *National Gardening*. Reporting on all aspects of home gardening, each issue is read by some half million gardeners worldwide.

For more information about the National Gardening Association, check out its Web site at www.garden.org or call 802-863-5251.

Dedication

To the memory of fellow-editor Walter Doty, whose creativity and work habits I've long aspired to and fallen short of, but whose deadline performance I may finally have matched in this book.

Authors' Acknowledgments

This book owes a lot to the efforts of a number of contributors. You don't think one person could possibly know all this stuff, do you?

Special thanks go to Lance Walheim, who wrote several chapters and supplied expertise especially on difficult, more technical material such as fertilizer, pests, weeds, and more. He did all this while writing an excellent book of his own, *Lawn Care For Dummies.*

Peggy Henry also made key contributions with chapters on maintenance. Valerie Easton deserves a lot of credit for her work on the design chapter and inspired designs themselves. Big thanks also to Barbara Pleasant, for her contribution to three chapters. For help with the regional section, I'm indebted to Carrie Chalmers and Nel Newman. Special thanks to Catherine Boyle, who compiled the frost-date chart.

The National Gardening Association thanks key participants at NGA: David Els, President; Michael MacCaskey, Editor-in-Chief, Bill Marken, For Dummies Series Editor, Larry Sommers, Associate Publisher; and Cahrlie Nardozzi, Senior Horticulturist. Special thanks to Suzanne DeJohn and Kathy Bond-Bori, NGA Staff Horticulturists, for their help.

Publisher's Acknowledgments

We're proud of this book; please send us your comments through our Dummies online registration form located at www.dummies.com/register/.

Some of the people who helped bring this book to market include the following:

Acquisitions, Editorial, and Media Development

Project Editor: Traci Cumbay

Acquisitions Editor: Kristin A. Cocks

Editorial Program Coordinator: Hanna K. Scott

Editorial Manager: Michelle Hacker

Editorial Supervisor and Reprint Editor: Carmen Krikorian

Editorial Assistant: Erin Calligan, David Lutton

Illustrations: Todd Sanders

Cover Photos: © Medioimages

Cartoons: Rich Tennant (www.the5thwave.com)

Composition Services

Project Coordinator: Kristie Rees

Layout and Graphics: Carl Byers, Joyce Haughey, Kathie Rickard, Brent Savage, Erin Zeltner

Proofreaders: Jessica Kramer

Indexer: Sherry Massey

Publishing and Editorial for Consumer Dummies

> **Diane Graves Steele,** Vice President and Publisher, Consumer Dummies
>
> **Joyce Pepple,** Acquisitions Director, Consumer Dummies
>
> **Kristin A. Cocks,** Product Development Director, Consumer Dummies
>
> **Michael Spring,** Vice President and Publisher, Travel
>
> **Kelly Regan,** Editorial Director, Travel

Publishing for Technology Dummies

> **Andy Cummings,** Vice President and Publisher, Dummies Technology/General User

Composition Services

> **Gerry Fahey,** Vice President of Production Services
>
> **Debbie Stailey,** Director of Composition Services

Contents at a Glance

Table of Contents

Introduction

Sure, you can live without annual flowers. You can also live without football, rainbow trout, Cabernet, and Boston terriers. But why should you?

Annuals are fun to grow for their brilliant colors, for their quick growth, for the life and spirit they add to a garden, for the butterflies and birds they attract, and for the way they can instantly transform something drab into a summer party place.

Growing annuals, of course, is not all fun and games. In this book, you can find plenty of advice on planting and taking care of the little guys. None of the caretaking involved is terribly tough, but following some basic steps can greatly increase your chance for satisfaction.

If I could take the secret to success with annuals and boil it down to three simple steps, those would be

✔ Choose the right plants for your garden's conditions (sun or shade, for example) and for your climate (mild or cold winters, for example).

✔ Plant them at the right time of year.

✔ Provide them with ongoing care.

I devote the rest of this book to expanding on these three steps.

About This Book

When the weather warms up, annuals begin spilling from window boxes and peeking out of containers, bringing color to fencelines and brightening lawns. They've long been a favorite because they're bright, relatively simple to grow, and reliably lovely.

To get great results from annuals, you don't need an advanced degree in horticulture, nor do you need to give up your weekends to tending your flower beds. However, knowing a few basics and putting forth the (minimal) effort required to apply them can make all the difference.

This book tells you only what you need to know to get great results from your annuals. You don't have to give up all your free time to grow a great garden, and you certainly don't have to give it up just to *read* about gardening.

How to Use This Book

This book is intended to serve readers in at least two typical situations. The way you approach gardening may influence how you approach this book:

- ✔ You go to the nursery, are seduced by the beauty of some geranium plants, and take them home with you. Now what to do? Pick up your trusty *Annuals For Dummies, Portable Edition* book and look up geraniums. Read about what you can expect from this plant, what conditions it needs, and any special care it may need. If you don't yet have a flower bed in which to plant your lovely new annuals, perhaps you turn to the chapter on preparing the soil (Chapter 6) and planting (Chapter 7) and, with luck, get your seedlings in the ground before they dry out. Later on, after your plants are safely growing and you have time, read up on watering, feeding, pest control, and other things you may need to know to care for the new additions to the family.

- ✔ The other type of reader is, shall I say, less impulsive. You want to know something about annuals before you start out. You read through the early chapters that discuss your climate and garden conditions (Chapters 2, 3, and 4), and you figure out what kinds of annuals best suit your needs. Read the plant descriptions in Chapter 5, study the color photographs, and choose the plants that most appeal to you. Figure out the watering (Chapter 8) and feeding (Chapter 9) schedules that will most benefit your new plants. If you're this kind of gardener, patient and conscientious, congratulations! I'm jealous of you. You will have a beautiful garden.

However you approach this book and whatever your level of experience, you're sure to find tips and information in these pages that will pay off in the garden.

Conventions Used in This Book

To help you navigate through this book, we've established the following conventions:

- ✔ *Italic* is used for emphasis and to highlight new words or terms that are defined.
- ✔ Monofont is used for Web addresses.
- ✔ Sidebars, which are shaded gray boxes full of text, consist of information that's interesting but not necessarily critical to your understanding of the topic.

Icons Used in This Book

Those cute little pictures in the margins of this book aren't just for decoration. They're pointing out some pretty important stuff.

Interested in environmentally friendly suggestions, like composting or conserving water? Look for this icon and do your part to keep the planet green.

As long as you're reading about how to grow beautiful flowers, why not pick up a few new words for your gardening vocabulary? Look for this icon when you want to make sense of the strange, new terms you encounter on seed packets, in catalogs, and at the garden center.

Almost everybody has a shady patch of yard where nothing seems to grow. This icon marks information about annuals that grow well in the shade, or other tips about accommodating shady spots.

All gardeners have their own bag of tricks. This icon marks nifty tips for growing better plants, saving money or time, or building a better garden.

If you're stuck on an island, you can plant a garden using nothing more than a sharpened stick. (Just ask Gilligan!) But having some basic tools makes your work a lot easier. And when you get serious about growing annuals, you can find some special equipment that will really show your garden who's the boss.

All things considered, gardening is a relatively safe pastime. However, it does have its hazards. This icon warns you of potential harm or injury to you or your plants from chemicals, pests, and other disasters of the flower world.

Where to Go From Here

Dig in anywhere you like! Unlike your high school algebra text, *For Dummies* books are made to be read in whatever order seems reasonable to you. So turn right to Chapter 6 if you want to find out about how to prepare your soil, or head to Chapter 12 if you need to find out how to rid your garden of pests.

"To our new neighbors. May you enjoy your new home, and keep your dog out of our flower beds."

Chapter 1

Friend to the Beginner, Challenge to the Expert

In This Chapter

▶ Ways in which annuals outshine other plants

▶ Bare-bone basics of garden jargon

▶ Seven rewarding projects for first-time gardeners to do with annuals

▶ Challenging ideas for veteran gardeners

*B*rilliantly colorful, yet short-lived. Perhaps this combination of qualities explains why people are so drawn to annuals, the shooting stars of the plant world, streaking across the summer in a burst of color and then burning out.

Even if you don't know what an annual is, you've no doubt seen plenty of them (although you probably just called them "flowers" instead of "annuals"). What many people recognize as the most familiar, friendliest flowers — petunias, marigolds, pansies, and the like — are actually annuals. The orange nasturtiums you see spilling out of window boxes, the yellow-and-white daisies sneaking up through cracks in the sidewalk, the pink hollyhocks standing tall next to grandma's chicken coop — these are the flowers of poetry, music, and fine art, or don't you remember Petunia Pig and Daisy Duck?

Why are annuals especially rewarding plants to grow? For a number of reasons:

- ✔ **Annuals are fun.** They exhibit the brightest, most endearing colors of the plant world.

- ✔ **Annuals are versatile.** You can grow them in beds, borders, pots, or baskets, in sun or shade, on top of bulbs, and underneath shrubs or trees.

✔ **Annuals don't mess around.** They grow fast and bloom young, even while they're still in little nursery packs. You can see what you're buying instead of having to wait for months until the blooms finally open. And, as a group, annuals give you more color for your money than any other plants.

✔ **Annuals respond to good care and let you know it.** When you provide the proper amount of water and fertilizer, annuals reward you with steady growth and a long bloom season. If you don't give your annuals the care they need, you'll usually know soon enough to replace your plants for that same season. Compare that quick feedback to planting an oak tree for your children to swing in and, years later, discovering that you've been stunting its growth. By that time, your kids have moved out of the house, blaming you for depriving them of the childhood pleasure of a tree swing.

Annuals are easy to grow and easygoing. Yet, they offer enough variety and complexity to challenge an expert gardener . . . and to fill the pages of this book.

What Makes a Plant an Annual?

To be technical for a moment, an *annual* is defined as a plant that undergoes its entire life cycle within one growing season, as illustrated in Figure 1-1. You plant a marigold seed in May, the seedling sprouts quickly, it starts blooming in July, frost kills it in October, seeds scatter and (with luck) sprout the next spring to start the process again. The good news is that nature typically blesses annuals with bright flowers to attract insects that will ensure pollination for seeds to sprout the next season.

Compare an annual with a *perennial.* By definition, a perennial is a plant that can live for several years, sprouting new growth and making new blooms year after year. Plant a typical perennial, such as columbine, from seed in May, and it spends the summer growing foliage, dies completely back to the ground when winter arrives, starts growing again the next spring, blooms that summer, dies back again, and repeats the pattern of blooming and dying back for years. (If you're interested in that kind of plant, too, pick up a copy of *Perennials For Dummies.*)

Also compare an annual to a *biennial,* which takes two years to bloom and complete its life cycle. In general, biennials grow only foliage for the first year and then bloom the second. However, some biennials can bloom in their first year if you plant the seeds early enough or if they happen to be one of the biennials bred for speed.

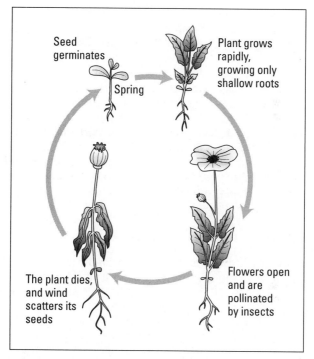

Seed germinates

Spring

Plant grows rapidly, growing only shallow roots

The plant dies, and wind scatters its seeds

Flowers open and are pollinated by insects

Figure 1-1: Annuals complete their entire life cycle, from seed to seed, in one year.

As gardening (if not life in general) has no doubt conditioned you to expect, these general rules do come with a couple of qualifications:

 ✔ Some plants that appear to be annuals are actually fast-growing biennials that can complete their two-year cycle in one year. For simplicity's sake, this book simply refers to such plants as annuals.

> ✔ Some perennials act like annuals when you grow them in cold climates. Ivy geraniums *(Pelargonium peltatum),* for example, may not survive the month of June in a climate with late frosts, such as Toronto, but will live longer than you do if planted in a mild climate, such as southern California. For the purposes of this book, I refer to such fair-weather perennials as annuals, as well.

Deciphering Gardenese

Okay, so gardeners don't have an entire language of their own. But when you start growing annuals, you soon encounter new words and jargon at the nursery, in catalogs, on seed packages, and even here, in a book that does its best to demystify garden-speak. Learning a bunch of gardening terminology may not seem important when you're wearing your gardening gloves and are itching to start digging, but knowing these terms makes your planting and growing experiences more pleasant and productive.

It's all in the name

You probably never refer to your family pet as a *Canis familiaris,* even though that's the official scientific term for the domesticated dog. In this tradition of classifying everything under the sun, plant experts created long Latin names for every known annual. Don't worry. In the real world, people rarely use these fancy names in place of a plant's perfectly good (though perhaps less accurate and certainly less impressive sounding) common name.

Every plant has a two-part botanical name, identifying its genus and species. The botanical name always appears underlined or in italics with the genus name (which appears first) capitalized; for example, *Tagetes erecta* is the botanical name for African marigold. The genus name (*Tagetes,* in this case), refers to a group of closely related plants found in nature. The species name (*erecta,* in this case), refers to a specific member of the genus — such as a tall, orange-flowered marigold.

Of course, most plants also have common names. But common names can vary from place to place and from time to time. *Nemophila menziesii* will always be the botanical name for the same plant, no matter where in the world you find it. But when it comes to this plant's common name, some people call it California bluebell, while others know it as baby blue eyes. To add to this confusion, different plants may share the same common name; various kinds of butterfly flowers exist, in addition to butterfly bush and butterfly weed. Sometimes the common name *is* the botanical name; for example, the botanical name for the petunia is *Petunia hybrida*.

You can see why people who want to be precise use the botanical names, but for most of us, and most of the time, common names work fine. And that's what we're going to use in this book. In case there might be confusion over a common name, check out the botanical name given in parentheses.

Some specialized plants have additional names tacked on to their botanical or common names:

- ✔ **Varieties and cultivars:** Many plants have another name, indicating a group of plants within a species that differ from the species in some particular way, such as flower color. When these subspecies occur naturally, they are called *varieties*. When the groups are manmade, they are referred to as *cultivars*. Variety names appear lowercased and italicized immediately after the species name, as in *Juniperus chinensis sargentii*. Cultivar names are capitalized and set apart in single quotes, as in *Tagetes erecta* 'Snowbird' — a white-flowered variety of marigold. Most of the annuals you see at nurseries or in seed catalogs are cultivars: 'Summer Sun' petunia, 'Freckles' geranium, or 'Pink Castle' celosia, for example.

- ✔ **Strains and series:** Another important player in the annuals name game is *strain* or *series*. These terms refer to a group of plants that share many similar growth characteristics but also differ among themselves in an important aspect. Many of the most popular annuals sold today are strains. Majestic Giant (note the lack of italics and quote marks) is a strain of pansies; all members of this strain develop similar big, blotchy flowers, but the blooms come in half a dozen different colors.

Flower shapes and plant sizes

Look what happens when expert plant breeders get their hands on annuals (or other flowering plants, for that matter): In nature, a flower may be yellow and have four petals. But after a few seasons under the guidance of a plant breeder, the same plant may produce a bloom with 16 white petals. Many flowers, but especially annuals, are highly malleable in these ways. Understanding all the whys and hows of plant size and shape isn't particularly important. Just remember that you can't expect a marigold, for example, to always look the same.

At nurseries, in seed catalogs, and in this book, you encounter specific names for certain kinds of flowers. Some examples appear in Figure 1-2 and in the following list:

- A *single* flower, which is the type most typical in nature, has a single layer of petals.

- A *double* flower has additional layers of petals, usually the result of breeding that has transformed some of the flower's other parts, such as sepals or stamens, into showy petals.

- A *bicolor* flower has two prominent colors in its petals. This flower type is similar to, but not the same as, the picotee.

- A *star* flower is absolutely no surprise: It has a star-shape.

- The tips of a *picotee* flower have a different color than the rest of the flower petals.

The rest of the annual, as well as its flowers, comes in a wide range of improvements. Most of the breeding efforts have been directed at smaller, more compact plants *(dwarfs)*, but you can also find many varieties developed to trail from hanging baskets *(trailers)*. Annuals that plant breeders have worked with for a long time (more than a hundred years with marigolds) show the widest range of plant forms. Marigolds have many, many varieties classified as tall, intermediate, and dwarf.

Hybrids: The pinnacle of the breeder's art

Today's flashy and dependable annuals owe a great deal to the hybridization efforts of plant breeders. A *hybrid* is the result of crossing two specific parent plants, such as a petunia with red and white flowers that results from crossing a red petunia with a white one.

An *F1 hybrid* is the result of crossing two carefully controlled parents to create seed that will grow into very predictable offspring. When you plant F1 hybrid seeds, you know exactly what they will grow into (a red and white petunia, for example). However, this second generation of plants won't produce seeds that grow into plants with the same predictability.

The predictable F1 hybrid qualities last only one generation. So this is the bottom line when you come across F1 hybrids: They cost more to develop and are priced higher at the nursery, but they offer benefits such as new flower colors, longer bloom season, bigger plants, or greater resistance to disease.

Hybrids are usually created in greenhouses where pollination can be carefully controlled. *Open pollination,* which occurs when annuals are grown in fields and allowed to be pollinated naturally by insects, yields far less predictable results than hybridization.

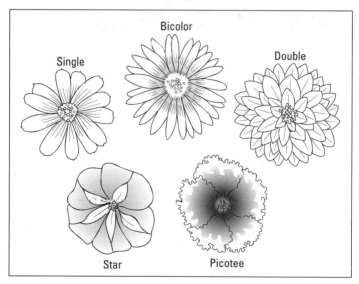

Figure 1-2: Flowers come in a range of shapes, sizes, and colors, including these favorites.

There they go, the All-Americas

What do the words *All-America Selections* (AAS) mean when they appear on a nursery label or alongside an annual described in a seed catalog?

In 1932, seed growers developed the All-America Selections program to recognize and promote outstanding new flower and vegetable creations. (Fleuroselect is the European equivalent of All-America Selections.) Each year, plant breeders enter new plant variations in the AAS competition, where they are grown at test gardens across North America. Judges look for improved qualities such as early bloom, disease or pest tolerance, new colors, novel flower forms, and longer bloom periods. The AAS logo on a plant indicates that it's a winner.

Over the years, more than 300 flowers have won AAS honors. Many are great; others have fallen by the wayside. Anytime you see the AAS symbol, you can feel pretty confident that the annual is well worth a try in your garden.

Rewarding Projects for Novice Gardeners

Go to any large garden center in June, and you find impatiens or petunias as far as the eye can see. These are universal flowers, loved by all, especially by beginners. You can't go wrong if you plant them at the right time of year in your climate and in the right conditions. But put impatiens in too sunny a spot, and you get tinder-dry kindling; plant impatiens too early, and frost will turn them into a pile of slime overnight.

Even if you've never grown anything before, you can create some wonderful effects with annuals just by keeping a few basics in mind. Try any of these projects with annuals, all of which are fairly easy to do and impressive in the garden:

> ✔ **Grow a sunflower taller than your rain gutter.** Children love growing sunflowers. The seeds are big enough to be easily grasped by pudgy, little fingers. Choose one of the monster-sized cultivars, such as 'Giganteus'. Plant the seeds directly in the ground in a sunny spot when the

weather warms up. Make sure that you water regularly and deeply. You may need to stake the plant; after all, it's growing 10 inches a week. In a few months, your family will be looking up at flower heads more than a foot wide.

✔ **Create a sophisticated color combination.** If you like gray and purple together as much as I do, this project will make you feel like a master color choreographer. Buy two or three nursery seedlings of dusty miller, a foliage plant with silver-gray leaves, and several seedlings of heliotrope, a plant blessed with deep purple, fragrant flowers and dark, glossy leaves. Pick a sunny spot and plant the heliotrope, which grows taller than dusty miller, in the back. Or combine two or three of each of the plants in a container at least 12 inches in diameter. The soft, gray dusty miller elegantly sets off the regal heliotrope colors.

✔ **Grow flowers for dinner.** Nasturtium flowers are colorful *and* edible — they make a peppery addition to any green salad. You can eat the whole nasturtium plant, but the tasty flowers are the best part.

✔ **Plant a flower bed in one step by sowing packs of seeds directly in the ground.** Take advantage of the fact that some annuals are easy to start from seeds. Marigolds and zinnias are noteworthy examples. Mix varieties in your flower bed or devote a bed to a single type. Prepare the planting bed by turning over the soil, raking it smooth, and preparing it as I describe in Chapter 6. Broadcast seeds evenly, cover them lightly with organic matter or soil mix, and keep them moist until seedlings are at least a couple inches tall. Thin the seedlings so they stand at the spacing recommended on the seed packet.

✔ **Bring in some instant color.** Sometimes, it's smart to pass up the tempting pots of annuals sold in full bloom at many nurseries. Plants this size can be expensive, and younger seedlings in smaller pots or packs can often catch up to and surpass them in just a few weeks. But how can you resist when you want the effect right away? To be smart about such extravagance, select "instant color" plants that have vigorous root systems. You can buy flower-covered geraniums, petunias, and pansies in 4-inch pots, gallon cans, or even larger containers; these plants perform better than most other annuals available at this size.

✔ **Grow bouquets of cut flowers.** A few rows of zinnias, sown directly in the ground in full sun at the back of your garden, can supply a summer's worth of cut flowers for your home. And here's something to feel good about: Zinnias benefit from cutting, which encourages more stems and flowers to develop.

✔ **Become a container maestro.** Growing annuals in containers can be a fascinating challenge that brings out the artist in you. But it can also be downright simple if you stick with surefire plants. Try this foolproof project for summer annuals: In late spring after frost danger, plant six impatiens seedlings in a 14-inch-diameter terra cotta bowl filled to within 1½ inches of the rim with commercial potting mix, keep the bowl in partial shade, water so soil is always moist, and fertilize monthly. For more information about container gardening, hike to your nearest bookstore and pick up a copy of *Container Gardening For Dummies* by Bill Marken and the Editors of the National Gardening Association.

For a colorful spring or early-summer combination, try yellow violas edged with sweet alyssum. Start with a 14-inch terra cotta bowl and commercial potting mix. Buy a six-pack each of violas and alyssum. Plant four of the violas in the center of the pot and surround them with two or three of the alyssum to spill over the sides. Grow in full sun. Use any leftover plants in other pots or transplant them into the ground.

✔ **Use foolproof plants.** If you are not sure what to plant, go to the nursery and buy what looks good from this list of good-looking, dependable annual flowers: cosmos, impatiens, lobelia, marigolds, nasturtium, petunias, portulaca, sweet alyssum, sweet William, and zinnias.

Challenging Projects for the Expert Gardener

Hundreds and hundreds of annuals are out there, so it's not surprising that among them are plenty of opportunities for anyone who wants to try something new and different. The following projects represent just a few of the more challenging adventures you can have with annuals. Proceed at your own speed.

✔ **Grow beautiful, old-fashioned bouquets.** Can anything match sweet peas for the nostalgic power of their perfume? But sweet peas are notoriously tricky to grow, subject to mildew, affected by hot weather (stems grow too short, flowers don't last), and afflicted by a host of infirmities. Sweet peas make you work for their beautiful fragrance, but it's worth it.

✔ **Grow a colorful annual border with no flowers.** Not all annuals use blooms to get their color. Coleus, for example, is an annual that's prized for its big, colorful leaves. Such nonflowering annuals are great for shady spots where flowers may not bloom well.

✔ **Create a 365-day border.** If you live in a mild-winter climate (such as much of California, low-elevation Arizona, and parts of the southern United States), you can have annuals in bloom every day of the year. The secret is to overlap plantings and be brutal about rotating plants. For example, if you have warm-season annuals still blooming in late summer, replace some of them with cool-season annuals — don't wait until the summer flowers are completely done, or you'll have a bare bed for a while. Remove the rest of the summer annuals when they finish blooming and move in more winter and spring annuals. This juggling act can get complicated. See Chapter 2 for suggestions for your climate.

✔ **Grow a hanging basket as big as your car.** Visitors to Victoria, the capital of British Columbia, Canada, are always amazed at the hanging baskets that decorate the city's lampposts. As one visitor put it, "They're so beautiful, I would have taken a couple home — except they were bigger than my car."

You can make a scaled-down version of these giant beauties by using a 16-inch wire basket, a cubic foot of sphagnum moss, and lightweight soil mix. You need about two dozen warm-season annuals: some that trail (such as ivy geraniums, lobelias, and petunias) and some that stand more upright (such as marigolds and schizanthus). Line the basket with moss and then fill it with soil mix to within 1½ inches of the top. Stuff trailing annuals into the sides of the basket and plant a few upright annuals in the center.

✔ **Grow rare tongue-twisters.** Schizanthus and salpiglossis are relatively unknown but decidedly attractive annuals. Actually, they're harder to spell than to grow, and they're well worth a try in your summer garden. If you're worried about pronunciation, just point at the nursery label.

✔ **Pamper a prima donna.** Transvaal daisy *(Gerbera)* is a truly beautiful annual with deeply colored, big, flatish, classic-daisy flowers on long, thick stems. It looks hard to grow . . . and it is. This plant requires perfect drainage, perfect weather, and perfect snail control. Are you up to the task? If not, you can do what I do: Buy blooming plants in 4-inch pots at the nursery, transplant extra carefully (the finicky Transvaal daisy is sensitive about transplanting, too) to a larger pot for about a month of glorious bloom on the front porch.

✔ **Take pride in your petunias.** Petunias are easy to grow from transplants, but really difficult to grow from seed. The seeds are about the size of dust, for one thing, and they demand a surprising amount of painstaking care. Why grow petunias from seed? You get a much bigger selection when you buy seeds instead of nursery transplants. And you get a great deal of satisfaction when you start with those dust specks in February and end up with blooming plants in July.

✔ **Coax a miracle from a patio crack.** Think of those unexpected details that make a garden special, like an African daisy poking up between flagstone slabs. Or, as in my garden, blue lobelia spilling from a pot holding a golden barrel cactus. How did I do it? I have no idea. Nature took care of it. Seeds from lobelias growing nearby made their way into the cactus pot, sprouted, found the spot to their liking, and now come back every year from the seeds of those before them.

Expert gardeners sometimes try duplicating nature by planting lobelia or African daisy seedlings between patio cracks, at the base of a brick planter, or in another situation that resembles a natural occurrence. With luck, the plants will adapt and reseed. But here's my big-picture advice that you won't find in fussbudget garden books: Take what nature gives you. Give those little sprouting plants a chance (unless you *know* they're weeds). Seedlings coming up on their own obviously are comfortable in that spot and may do better than anything you intentionally plant there. Tolerate a little disorder and plant improvisation among your annuals.

Chapter 2

Growing Annuals in Your Little Corner of the World

In This Chapter

▶ Enjoying warm-season and cool-season annuals

▶ Knowing when to plant what

▶ Assessing the conditions in your garden

*I*f you plant annuals at the right season and in the right spot in your garden, you can easily have months of glorious blooms. But if you start a marigold too early, place a zinnia in a spot that's too shady, or stick a begonia where it's too dry, you'll get a quick lesson in the importance of understanding your garden's climate patterns and other conditions. (In case you're curious, the results of the unwise plantings suggested in the previous sentence are a blackened, frost-burned marigold; a lanky, bloomless zinnia; and begonia toast.)

Before you head to the nursery to buy your plants, first try to find out a few things about your area's climate and seasons, plus some of your own garden's special conditions. Armed with that knowledge, you can make much wiser selections at planting time and give your annuals a much better chance of flourishing.

What You Do (And Don't) Need to Know about Your Climate

To grow annuals, you don't need to worry about your precise climate zone and temperature extremes as much as you do with permanent plants, such as perennials, trees, and shrubs. If you want to grow roses, for example, you need to know whether the temperature in your area drops to 10°F (–12°C) or –10°F (–23°C). That temperature difference can affect which roses adapt to your area.

Annuals are more straightforward. You simply have to wait until after the last killing frost to plant. (Use Table 2-1 as a predictor, or contact your local weather bureau or cooperative extension service for an idea of the date of the last killing frost in your area.) In fact, no matter where you live, you can probably wait until the first of June to plant impatiens and feel comfortable that you're doing the right thing at the right time for your climate. But if you take this "safe" approach to gardening, you miss a lot of the fun of growing annuals. By experimenting with a variety of annuals, you reap the rewards: flowers that bloom as long as your seasons allow, and flowers that bloom in all the different spots in your garden.

Even though annuals live for only one season, you want to make those few months as pleasant as possible for them. That means planting at the right time in your region.

Table 2-1	Frost Dates and Length of Growing Season		
City	**Last Frost in Spring**	**First Frost in Fall**	**Length of Growing Season**
Birmingham, Alabama	March 19	November 14	240 days
Phoenix, Arizona	January 28	December 16	322 days
Little Rock, Arkansas	March 17	November 10	238 days

City	Last Frost in Spring	First Frost in Fall	Length of Growing Season
Los Angeles, California	*	*	288 days
Santa Ana, California	*	*	338 days
Denver, Colorado	May 3	October 16	166 days
New Haven, Connecticut	April 15	October 27	195 days
Dover, Delaware	April 15	October 26	194 days
Miami, Florida	none	none	365 days
Orlando, Florida	January 31	December 17	320 days
Atlanta, Georgia	March 21	November 18	242 days
Boise, Idaho	May 6	October 12	159 days
Chicago, Illinois	April 8	November 9	215 days
Indianapolis, Indiana	April 17	October 27	193 days
Des Moines, Iowa	April 19	October 22	186 days
Wichita, Kansas	April 5	November 1	210 days
Louisville, Kentucky	April 1	November 7	220 days
New Orleans, Louisiana	February 13	December 12	302 days

(continued)

Table 2-1 *(continued)*

City	Last Frost in Spring	First Frost in Fall	Length of Growing Season
Portland, Maine	*	*	136 days
Baltimore, Maryland	March 26	November 19	238 days
Boston, Massachusetts	April 5	November 8	217 days
Detroit, Michigan	April 24	October 22	181 days
Minneapolis, Minnesota	April 30	October 13	166 days
Jackson, Mississippi	March 10	November 13	248 days
St. Louis, Missouri	April 3	November 6	217 days
Billings, Montana	May 15	September 24	132 days
Lincoln, Nebraska	April 20	October 17	180 days
Las Vegas, Nevada	March 13	November 13	245 days
Concord, New Hampshire	May 11	September 30	142 days
Newark, New Jersey	April 3	November 8	219 days
Albuquerque, New Mexico	April 16	October 29	196 days
New York City, New York	April 7	November 12	219 days
Charlotte, North Carolina	March 21	November 15	239 days

City	Last Frost in Spring	First Frost in Fall	Length of Growing Season
Fargo, North Dakota	May 13	September 27	137 days
Cincinnati, Ohio	April 15	October 25	192 days
Oklahoma City, Oklahoma	March 28	November 7	224 days
Portland, Oregon	February 25	December 1	279 days
Pittsburgh, Pennsylvania	April 16	November 3	201 days
Providence, Rhode Island	April 13	October 27	197 days
Charleston, South Carolina	February 19	December 10	294 days
Rapid City, South Dakota	May 7	October 4	150 days
Memphis, Tennessee	March 20	November 12	237 days
Dallas, Texas	March 18	November 12	239 days
Houston, Texas	February 4	December 10	309 days
Salt Lake City, Utah	April 12	November 1	203 days
Burlington, Vermont	May 8	October 3	146 days
Richmond, Virginia	*	*	206 days
Seattle, Washington	February 23	November 30	280 days
Petersburg, West Virginia	April 30	October 5	158 days

(continued)

Table 2-1 (continued)

City	Last Frost in Spring	First Frost in Fall	Length of Growing Season
Milwaukee, Wisconsin	April 20	October 25	188 days
Cheyenne, Wyoming	May 20	September 27	130 days

* Data not available
Based on "Climates of the States," by the National Oceanic and Atmospheric Administration

Use Table 2-1 to calculate another important feature of your climate: the length of the *growing season*. The growing season is simply the typical number of days between spring's last frost and fall's first frost. Generally, the farther north you are, the shorter your growing season. Growing-season length can be a factor when you're choosing annuals, especially from seed catalogs, which list the number of days to bloom.

Days to bloom is an important number for annuals. It's usually listed right on the seed packet or in the seed catalog, sometimes right after the plant name. Specifically, this figure refers to the number of days a plant requires after you plant its seed for the flower to bloom. But this number is an average, not an absolute. The actual number of days a plant takes to bloom in your garden may be more or less, depending on your climate and weather. Your goal is to determine whether a plant's days-to-bloom average fits comfortably within your growing season. If your growing season is 100 days long, and a flower takes, on average, 120 days to bloom, pass it by. If you absolutely must have this flower in your garden, start the seeds indoors a month or more before the last frost.

Warm-Season versus Cool-Season Annuals

The first question to ask about any annual that you'd like to add to your garden is not "What's its zodiac sign?" but "Is it a

warm-season or a cool-season annual?" Understanding the difference is vital to planting annuals at the right time of year in
your area.

Depending on their origin and what's been bred into them, different annuals prefer different conditions. Fortunately, for
those who have trouble remembering the growing requirements of every flower, you can focus on only two main categories of annuals: cool season and warm season.

Cool season and *warm season* are, of course, relative terms.
Where summers are cool, such as along the foggy California
coast or other overcast climates, you can grow cool-season
annuals all summer. Where winters are warm and nearly frost-
free, such as in low-elevation Arizona, fall through spring is an
ideal time to grow cool-season annuals like Iceland poppies
and stock, and even some warm-season annuals like petunias.
In fact, winter and early spring make up the main flower-growing
season in Arizona — summer there is too hot to grow any
annuals except the most heat-tolerant warm-season varieties.

If you live where summers are hot, which is most of the
United States, plant cool-season annuals as early as possible
(even before the last spring frost), and replace them after they
fade in hot weather. If you live where summers are hot and
winters are *relatively* mild (not dropping too far below freezing), you can plant these cool-season annuals in the fall, leave
them over the winter, and they'll bloom in early spring.

The cool cats

Cool-season annuals are those that perform best when temperatures are mild — about 70°F (21°C) — days are short, and
soil is cool. In most parts of the United States and Canada,
these conditions are typical in early spring and early fall.
Temperatures may be similarly mild all season in mountain
regions or in regions to the far north (or the far south, in the
Southern Hemisphere). In some coastal regions, temperatures
stay mild year-round.

Cool-season annuals can stand a varying amount of frost, from
a little to a lot; some types, in fact, are quite hardy and are
actually perennials that live through the winter in many areas.
The enemies are hot weather and long days, which cause

cool-season annuals to produce fewer blooms and ultimately die. Examples of cool-season favorites are calendulas, pansies, and snapdragons.

You're usually safe planting cool-season annuals a few weeks before the average date of the last spring frost in your area. If you live where weather is cool year-round or during the growing season, plant mostly cool-season annuals. If you live where summer days are hot and winters are mild, such as Phoenix, Palm Springs, or the Gulf Coast, plant cool-season annuals in the fall for a winter garden.

In the typical cold-winter/hot-summer climate, the time to plant cool-season annuals is early spring — from four to eight weeks before the typical last frost or as soon as the ground can be worked (dug and turned over). Their season ends with the arrival of hot weather, when you can replace them with warm-season annuals. Where summers rarely heat up, many cool-season annuals can thrive all summer right alongside warm-season annuals that don't demand hot weather.

Some like it hot

Warm-season annuals are those that thrive in hot summer weather. Most are tender and get damaged or downright destroyed by freezing temperatures. Examples are celosias, marigolds, vinca rosea (also called Madagascar periwinkle), and zinnias. Plant these heat-seekers after soil and air temperatures begin to warm up, and expect them to reach their peak in midsummer.

So what is the magic date to plant warm-season annuals? That depends on your climate. (Bet you knew I was going to say that!) Suppose, for example, that you live in the most typical climate, the one that predominates over most of the northern United States, Canada, and northern Europe. This climate typically has cold winters (usually with snow) and warm, often humid summers. In this climate, you can generally grow warm-season annuals from late spring through late summer or early fall.

The basic rule for planting: Wait until the danger of frost has passed — by then, the weather is usually also warming enough for growth and blooming.

To determine frost-safe planting dates in your area, refer to Table 2-1. Based on long-term weather records, the chart shows the average dates of the last frost of the spring and the first frost of the fall. To find the planting date for warm-season annuals, take the last date of spring frost in an area near you or in an area with a climate similar to yours and add ten days, to be safe. (Or be ready to protect plants with floating row covers.)

Floating row covers are an essential tool for gardeners who want to squeeze every bit of warmth out of early spring or late fall weather. Several types are available, but all share two traits: They are porous and very lightweight. You can lay floating row covers right over tender growing plants without smothering or crushing them. More importantly, these covers provide just enough insulation to protect plants on those clear, chilly nights when plants are most likely to suffer frost damage.

The date of the last frost is not the only guideline to use when planting annuals. For example, what if you want to grow warm-season annuals in mild-winter climates? If you live in southern California and follow the chart, for example, you might assume that you can plant zinnias in January. Frost isn't a threat then, but January temperatures aren't warm enough to encourage growth. Warm-season annuals need warm temperatures as well as frost-free conditions. Plant when the weather starts to warm up a bit. See more specific dates in Chapters 3 and 4. Note that some warm-season annuals need more heat than others.

Focusing on Your Garden

Before you plant, observe the conditions in your garden. Keep the following factors in mind when considering which annuals to plant and where to plant them.

Sun or shade

Plants have natural attributes that enable them to perform better in certain amounts of sunlight. Think about a plant's heredity for a few seconds. Where would a vine native to the jungle grow best in a garden? Probably where it receives some protection from the sun, such as under a high canopy of trees, similar to the shelter that it receives in its native habitat. Give the vine too much sun, and its foliage burns like the skin of an Irish redhead on the beach at Cancun. Or consider a plant with a sunny heredity. Zinnias, originally from Mexico, thrive in full sun. In too much shade, they grow spindly and develop mildew on their leaves.

Most annuals do best in *full sun.* That usually means about seven hours of sunlight during a summer day. Those hours should come during the middle of the day. If a spot in the garden gets its seven hours during the morning or late afternoon when the sun is not as intense, that location probably is not sunny enough for most sun-loving annuals. In those areas, you can plant shade-lovers such as impatiens or begonias.

Try to notice the pattern of sun and shade in your garden. It changes with time and the seasons: as the sun moves higher and lower in the sky, as trees grow taller and develop and lose leaves, and as neighbors build or tear down buildings.

Do you live in an all-year climate for annuals?

In some places, you can grow annuals all year. Winter temperatures rarely drop much below freezing in these regions, which include California (except for higher elevations), low elevations of the Southwest, and milder sections of the South, such as the Gulf Coast.

In mild-climate regions, you can plant cool-season annuals, such as lobelia and Iceland poppies, in late summer or early fall (after summer cools off). Blooms may appear before Christmas and peak in late winter and early spring. After growth and flowering slow down in spring, replace the cool-season annuals with warm-season annuals.

In mild climates, cool-season annuals can also be planted through the winter and early spring. They miss out on fall's warm weather to push them into growth but surge as soon as temperatures start to warm in late winter and early spring. See Chapters 3 and 4 for planting dates in your region.

Truly tropical climates, such as those found in Hawaii and southern Florida, are in a separate category and have their own special guidelines for growing annuals. If you live in a tropical climate, check with local nurseries for advice.

The following terms may help you determine what kind of sunlight your garden has:

- ✔ A northern exposure probably is blocked from the sun all day. This is *full shade.*

- ✔ The east side of your house, unless it's blocked by trees or buildings, probably gets sun in the morning and shade for the rest of the day. This is a typical *part shade* setting.

- ✔ A southern exposure gets the most hours of sun — this is *full sun.*

- ✔ A western exposure may get shade in the morning and full sun in the afternoon — this usually should be considered a sunny location because of the intensity of the light. (Shade plants will probably cook there.)

Pay attention to the sun/shade requirements specified for each plant. And watch the flowers that you plant to see how they respond. Signs of too much sun include brown, burned spots on the leaves. Results of too much shade include spindly foliage growth and weak blooming. If you notice those signs, experiment with different plants next time.

Definitions of sun and shade also depend on your climate. For example, near a coast, where it's cool and often overcast, plants generally need more sun than do plants in inland regions. In these cool, cloudy regions, sun-loving plants, such as zinnias, may have trouble growing even in direct sun, and plants that prefer shade, such as begonias, can come out from the shadows to flourish in full sun.

Wind

Will annuals be exposed to wind in your garden? Wind can dry out the soil quickly and rob plants of moisture. Stiff breezes can topple tall plants and break brittle ones. Although you can't do much about the wind, you *can* make sure that you water carefully. Planting shrubs or trees to provide a windbreak also may help. Or you may have to simply find a more protected spot for your annuals.

Soil

You may be stuck with soil that drains poorly or that otherwise makes life tough for annuals. Chapter 6 tells you how to know what kind of soil you have and, if it's lousy, how to improve it.

Slope

Gardening on a hillside presents some special challenges — watering is more difficult, for one thing. Terracing and drip irrigation are ways to ensure that enough moisture gets to plant roots.

Drip irrigation is a very slow and precise way to water plants. This method is great on slopes because the water is applied so slowly that it has time to actually soak in and not run off. Chapter 8 includes more information about drip irrigation.

Hilly terrain also can affect weather conditions. A sunny, south-facing slope can provide a milder situation for annuals because cold air drains away. You may find a hillside garden to be several degrees warmer and several weeks ahead of the neighbor's garden at the bottom of the hill.

Reflected heat

Pavement, house walls, and other heat-reflective surfaces can warm up a garden. Although these surfaces can be positive factors under certain conditions, reflected heat usually causes plants to burn up. Before you plant, be aware of conditions that are too bright — for example, the pavement around a swimming pool. Unless your plants can take intense heat, you're better off planting them somewhere with a little more shade.

Many annuals thrive on sun and heat. If you want to plant in a hot spot, consider such old favorites as petunias and marigolds, as well as lesser-known annuals such as Mexican sunflower and strawflowers.

Chapter 3

Month by Month in the Northern or Southern States

* *

In This Chapter

▶ Calendars for growing annuals in two distinct climate regions

▶ Suggestions for plants that may work well where you live

▶ A time to plant, a time to sow, a time to prune, a time to grow . . .

* *

*T*he calendars in this chapter and Chapter 4 can help you do all the right things for your annuals at the right time. They show you the best months for planning the garden, preparing the soil, sowing seeds, planting seedlings, cutting and weeding, controlling pests, doing cleanup, and performing other chores. They even list the best times to simply kick back and admire your handiwork.

Because annuals are fairly easy to grow (ranging somewhere between a plastic tulip and a rhododendron in difficulty), these calendars of advice are on the simple side. I divide the United States and much of Canada into big annual-growing regions. You can use this simplified system, rather than the complicated 11-climate USDA zone map, because annuals don't need to survive cold winters year after year the way permanent plants must.

If you don't see your region here, check Chapter 4. If you live in a country other than the United States or Canada, follow the advice of a climate region in this chapter that comes close to yours — northern Europe, for example, compares most closely with the northern belt of the United States, and Great Britain's climate is similar to the Pacific Northwest's.

Even though this chapter is relatively simple, climates are, by nature, complex, and weather varies from year to year. Weather is also local, with big swings in cold, heat, rain, snow, and almost everything else occurring over just a few miles. So use the calendars in this chapter as a guideline, but continue looking to the skies, checking the thermometer, and talking to the friendly folks at your local nursery to make sure that you're on the right track.

Calendar for the North: Warm Summers, Cold Winters

People tend to think of the northeastern, northern, and mid-western sections of the United States and Canada as separate regions and growing climates. True, these regions encompass a diverse range of climates and gardening conditions. In northern New England, winter temperatures may dip to –40°F (–40°C), whereas regions of the lower Midwest, such as southern Kansas and Missouri, may not experience temperatures lower than –10°F (–23°C).

For the purposes of this chapter, however, I group all these regions together, along with most of Canada. (British Columbia falls in the Pacific Northwest region, which I cover in Chapter 4.) This is possible because the most important concern for growing annuals is not how cold the winter gets, but rather when the first and last frosts of the growing season are likely to occur. The frost dates determine seeding schedules, planting times, duration of garden chores, and the ability to grow fall-blooming annuals. Check the listing of frost dates and season lengths in Chapter 2 to get a more precise idea of when to start annuals and how long the growing season is in your area.

Despite their diversities, all these regions share your basic North American weather: warm summers and cold winters. You won't find annuals growing during the winters in this region; they'd have to hide under a blanket of snow or endure subzero temperatures. The main season for annuals begins with planting time in early or midspring and ends when serious frosts hit in the fall.

January

Settle next to the fire with a stack of new seed catalogs. Starting your own annuals from seed can save money, provide a greater selection of varieties and colors, and become a satisfying spring ritual for you.

February

Prepare a space for starting seeds if you haven't already done so. Clear an area in a sunny window or set up fluorescent lights for seedlings to sprout and grow. Buy seed-starting trays or use old trays that you've cleaned with a dilute bleach solution and rinsed well. Consider providing bottom heat, which maintains an even, warm soil temperature and improves germination; many mail-order catalogs offer heating mats specifically for seed starting.

Use a commercial potting mix for starting seeds: a fine germinating mix for tiny seeds, and a coarser, peat-based mix for larger seeds and for growing your seedlings on to maturity.

March

March through mid-April is seed-starting time in cold climates. Plan a seeding schedule — essential in short-season climates where you want to make every day count. Start by figuring out when you want to transplant annuals into the ground in the weeks and months ahead, and work backward to calculate the best time to sow the seeds indoors. In most cases, you need to plant four to eight weeks ahead of transplanting time, depending on how long it takes seeds to reach transplanting size. For instance, if you can plant petunias outdoors in your area in mid-May (after frost danger) and petunia seeds take eight weeks to reach transplanting stage after sowing, you should start the seeds indoors around March 15.

April

You still have time to sow seeds indoors for transplanting next month — especially in colder climates where winters are most severe and the growing season is shortest. If your last-frost date falls around Memorial Day, you should sow seeds for all annuals, except fast-growing, tender plants (cosmos and zinnias, for example), by mid-April.

Watch indoor seedlings for pests and diseases. Plants infested with aphids often exhibit curled leaves and a shiny, sticky substance on their leaves; look under the leaves for clusters of aphids. A soap solution is an effective way to kill aphids, but you must apply it thoroughly and regularly until the population is under control. Try to avoid the conditions that encourage aphids: poor air circulation, overcrowding, and overfertilizing. Damping off is a common disease that affects new seedlings; sprouts rot near soil level and collapse. Prevent this disease by using a sterile soil mix and not overwatering. (See Chapter 12 for more information on pests and diseases.)

If you live in warmer areas with milder winters, you can start sowing seeds of hardy annuals directly into the ground a couple weeks before the last frost date in your region. If it's still cold in April where you live, wait until next month to direct-sow seeds. Hardy annuals that are easy and productive when sown directly include calendula, cornflower, larkspur, and poppies. Make sure that the ground is workable and not too wet.

Here's a good test to determine when your ground is ready: Form some garden soil into a ball and drop it from waist-high distance. It should break apart easily when it hits the ground. If it does not crumble apart, the soil is still too wet to plant, and seeds are likely to rot if sown directly into the ground.

If you plant nothing else, sow sweet pea seeds as soon as the ground can be dug. They appreciate the early start — especially if they can bloom before hot weather.

Depending on your region, late April or May is the time to lay out beds and prepare the soil. Adjust the soil pH based on soil tests done in the fall. Amend the soil with a 2- or 3-inch layer of organic matter and a complete fertilizer. (See Chapters 6 and 9 for more details.)

May

Early May is usually the best time to plant hardy annuals (seeds or transplants) in most areas — 10 to 14 days before the last frost is usually safe. Check local garden centers for the following ready-to-plant cool-season annuals: calendula, cornflower, pansies, snapdragons, stock, and violas. Look for stocky, green plants when shopping at garden centers. Avoid plants with dead lower leaves and brown, overcrowded roots, as well as plants that are already flowering.

This month begins the main season for transplanting into the ground tender annuals, such as impatiens, lobelia, and petunias. Wait until frost danger has passed, the soil and air have warmed up, and the nights are no longer cold. Memorial Day is considered optimum timing for planting tender annuals in many places. Tender plants set out too early may not be damaged by frost, but they don't grow during cold weather.

If you start seeds indoors, be sure to *harden off* (acclimate) transplants before planting them in the garden. Allow the plants to dry slightly and move them outdoors to a sheltered, shady location for a few days. Gradually move them into full sun and exposure to the elements. Transplant the toughened plants into a prepared bed.

Gardeners in warmer areas of the North can sow seeds of zinnias, morning glories, and cosmos directly in the ground as the weather heats up. In the coldest parts of the North, it makes sense to use transplants, except for sunflowers, which can be direct-seeded easily in most areas.

When seedlings sown directly in the ground reach 2 inches high, thin them according to the spacing recommended for each variety.

Beware of rogue frosts. Especially on clear, cold nights, be ready to cover young transplants with a *cloche* (a transparent plastic or glass cover) or lightweight row covers. Also watch for cutworm damage to direct-seeded crops and young transplants; cutworms wrap around the base of seedlings and chew through the stems. A damaged plant appears to be cut by a knife, with the top lying on the ground. Dig around the base of the plant to find the rolled-up grub and destroy it. If the problem is severe, fashion a 2-inch collar of tar paper or cardboard and wrap it around the stem of the plant so that the collar extends into the ground.

June

Continue planting tender annuals according to the guidelines that I describe for May. Old-timers in cold, mountainous areas (such as parts of Vermont) often wait until June 10 to plant the most tender plants, such as impatiens, because cold nights early in the month stress heat-lovers.

Newly planted seeds and transplants are vulnerable. Pay attention to their needs. Water if June is dry. Weeds compete for nutrients and water; hoe or pull the weeds while they are young and easy to remove. Watch for cutworms, slugs, and aphids that can stunt plants.

Mulch to conserve water and slow weed growth. Pull off fading blooms of cool-season annuals to extend their season of color. Pinch back impatiens, petunias, snapdragons, and zinnias to stimulate a branching, bushy habit.

July

July brings hot, dry weather, when plants require extra water and nutrients to keep them at their peak. Container-bound plants, particularly, suffer from heat stress and usually need daily watering if they're located in the sun. Container gardens quickly deplete soil nutrients; feed window boxes and pots with a liquid fertilizer every couple weeks.

Continue feeding annuals to promote steady growth for the remainder of the summer. Stake taller annuals, such as larkspur, cornflower, cosmos, and nicotiana. Deadhead flowers regularly. You can shear some annuals, such as alyssum and lobelia, to encourage them to bloom again in a few weeks. In hot climates, cool-season annuals probably have peaked, so pull them out.

Japanese beetles make an appearance toward the end of the month. Hand-pick bugs and drop them into a container of soapy water.

August

In northern regions where the growing season is 90 to 110 days long, late July through early August is the garden's peak. It's called "high summer" because so many kinds of plants are blooming all at once. Enjoy the fruits of your work and remember to make notes for next year.

Some late-summer tasks to keep you busy:

✔ Continue to deadhead, water, and weed. Containers, especially, still need to be fertilized.

✔ Tidy beds and containers by pulling out plants that have been crowded out or have passed their peak.

✔ Harvest flowers for drying and enjoy fresh-cut bouquets. You can't go wrong with fresh-cut bouquets of 'Rocket' snapdragons and 'Cut and Come Again' zinnias.

✔ Keep picking Japanese beetles. Drop them into a container of soapy water. (See Chapter 12 for more information on these and other garden pests.)

September

Listen to weather reports and be ready with row covers or blankets if an early frost is predicted and you still have tender plants in bloom. You can place bushel baskets over clumps of plants, or you can cover whole beds with sheets.

Collect seed pods, dried flowers, and grasses to make arrangements.

You can pot some annuals — begonias, coleus, impatiens, and geraniums — and bring them indoors. If plants are lanky by summer's end, cut stems back by about a third. Place pots in a sunny window or under grow-lights. Water and fertilize less frequently than you did when the plants were in the ground. Plants seem to need a resting phase after a summer of blooming.

October

Pull out dead plants and add them to your compost pile. If your compost from the summer is almost decomposed, start a new compost pile of garden debris and leaves. Next spring, spread the decomposed pile on your beds and add new debris to the pile started in the fall.

Take soil samples in the fall to know how to amend soil next spring. Use the results of the soil tests to gauge any adjustments that you need to make in soil pH and fertility. Refer to Chapter 6 for more information about amending soil.

November through December

Sharpen, clean, and oil your tools. Keep a record of any extra seed you have. Store the extra seed in an airtight container in a cool location; add packets of silica gel to absorb any moisture in the container. Build your own window boxes or trellises for next year. Build a cold frame for growing and hardening off your transplants.

A *cold frame* is a low box open to the soil but with a "skylight" of glass or plastic on the top. Like a miniature greenhouse, cold frames provide just enough protection from wind and cold to get plants off to a faster start or to acclimate them to outdoors.

Sort through your notes from the summer and determine what flowers, planting schedules, and gardening practices were successful and decide what areas need improvement. Seek inspiration in books and magazines. Think about what appeals to you when you respond to a photograph of a beautiful garden: Is it the color, the fullness, the simplicity, or the variety?

Calendar for the South: Hot Summers, Mild Winters

The South, as defined in this calendar, ranges from the mountains of North Carolina to just above the tropical tip of south Florida, and from Dallas, Texas, to Savannah, Georgia. Weather may move in from the Midwest, but the region is more often affected by the adjacent oceans and the jet stream's prevailing winds. From north to south, the dates of first and last frosts in this region differ by a month to six weeks — these dates, of course, help you determine when to plant annuals.

This calendar's timing aims for the middle south in the middle of each month. For the lower south, the tasks will fall toward the beginning of the month. For the upper south, wait until month's end. Tropical Florida (Dade County south to the Keys) has its own rules for planting annuals, which are unlike the guidelines for any other gardening region in the continental United States. If you live in tropical Florida, check with local experts for recommended varieties and planting times.

January

Keep pansy blossoms plucked to get more buds and blooms. Remember that winter annuals grow while all else lies dormant, so fertilize garden beds and containers of annuals when you're watering this month.

The best seeds to start indoors now to plant outdoors in six to eight weeks are ageratum, coleus, cosmos, dusty miller, love-lies-bleeding, nicotiana, salvia, and wishbone flower. Use this simple seed-starting system: Plant seeds in flats of sterile soil mix and put them on top of the refrigerator or clothes dryer next to a sunny window. The bottom heat hastens seed sprouting.

Make the most of a wet, warm day to get rid of winter weeds. Pulling even tiny oak trees is a no-sweat job in this type of weather.

Take advantage of breaking weather to work the soil for spring planting. Turn the soil over with shovel or tiller as described in Chapter 6, add organic matter and a complete fertilizer, and then let it mellow till March.

February

If seedlings recently sown indoors look skinny, they probably need more light. Add a fluorescent lamp or move flats closer to the light source.

As soon as possible, plant early spring annuals, including petunias and geraniums. If those don't grow over the winter in your area, look for Canterbury bells, delphinium, foxglove, larkspur, and snapdragons to transplant.

Start a garden journal to record what and when you plant, whether it bloomed, what bugs bugged you, and which fungus invaded your garden. Knowledge is (flower) power.

Put up a trellis ahead of time to support vigorous vines for summer shade. Use wood, plastic, iron, or bent native wood; anchor legs in 4 inches of concrete.

March

Transplant ageratum, begonia, lobelia, love-lies-bleeding, and nicotiana to slightly shady spots. Plant cosmos, dusty miller, marigolds, and annual verbena in warm, sunny beds or pots. Water transplants well and feed them with fish emulsion or root-stimulator fertilizer, following the directions on the label.

Sow the seeds of the *Ipomoea* family (including cardinal climber, moonflower, and morning glory) and love-in-a-puff

(Cardiospermum haliacacabum) directly where they'll grow. Plant big-seeded annuals such as globe amaranth, sunflowers, zinnias and in small pots.

If you've had trouble starting seeds in the garden, try this: Top your garden soil with an inch of potting soil or compost. Seeds planted in this way still may dry out before sprouting, however, so lay a board on top to hold in the moisture, just until they sprout.

Make sure that young poppies and larkspur don't dry out; as they put on flower buds, it's okay to water and mulch around the base of the plants. Gently pull the mulch away from pansies and other transplants tucked in last fall.

Make patio pots work overtime: Combine tomato and basil plants with calliopsis, coleus, and marigolds for food plus flowers for the table.

Slugs and snails destroy tender transplants. Limit their numbers by working *diatomaceous earth* (powdery, sharp-edged skeletal remains of tiny sea creatures called *diatoms*) into the top inch of the bed before transplanting.

April

The soil's warming up across the South, so add mulch around spring annuals and don't forget to apply fertilizer and thoroughly water the flowers you transplanted last month.

April is the time to deadhead spring flowers for a second round of flowers; if you allow the seeds to set, the plant's done for the year.

Impatiens are the top transplant this month. You can choose from traditional single flowers or hot, new double blossoms. If your shade is too dense for flowers, nestle pots of impatiens into ground covers.

Coleus is better than ever, with varieties adapted for full sun or part shade. For bushier plants, pinch the third set of leaves that emerges. Those pinched-off stems root easily in water or wet sand.

Now is also the time to plant some of the following up-and-coming annuals: *Angelonia, Bacopas, Evolvulus* 'Blue Daze', *Felicia, Linaria* 'Fantasy', petunia 'Purple Wave', and *Scaevola.*

May

Spider mites and aphids arrive to eat the most tender shoots, but they're slow buggers that dislike water. Water regularly with a sprinkler to discourage both insects.

Plant the following summer annuals from seed directly where you want them to grow: celosia, Mexican sunflower, spider flower, sunflowers, and zinnia.

When night temperatures climb, pansies and violas respond with smaller flowers and skinnier stems. May is the time to make compost of them.

Look for vinca rosea (sold as annual periwinkle in many Southern nurseries) in varieties bred for disease resistance. Don't plant them until this month at the earliest. Natives of Madagascar, vincas thrive where it's hot and dry.

For pure cottage-garden flair, combine cosmos with zinnias. Unfortunately, both flowers can suffer from leaf spot early and powdery mildew later. To keep leaves looking good, thin plants to stand 4 inches apart and do not mulch.

June

After your transplants are in the ground and your seedlings are up and growing, you need to be watching for signs of trouble. One common warning flag is yellow leaves on young plants. Here's an almost foolproof backyard diagnosis: Yellow lower leaves indicate a need for nitrogen, and yellow leaves at the growing point signal a root problem or that the flower was planted too deep.

New Guinea impatiens are great plants for many locations in your garden, and June is the time to plant them. They tolerate sun or shade, lots of fertilizer or just a little, and life in pots or in beds, but they do not tolerate drought and high temperatures. Water these plants in the containers before setting them out in the garden.

Transplant begonia, bluebell, and wishbone-flower seedlings to shady gardens. Their colors and textures bring welcome contrast to impatiens.

To fertilize beds in dry spells, water them first and then use a fertilizer mixed with more water. Make sure that the water soaks through thick mulches; rake back a bit of mulch if you must or, better yet, use soaker hoses.

July

Plant the second round of heat-loving summer annuals: balsam, celosia, cockscombs, marigolds, and zinnias. Include some of the following "bounce-back" flowers that recover quickly after thunderstorms: dwarf sunflowers, Mexican sunflower, portulaca, scaevola, and vinca rosea.

Off with their heads! Cut back impatiens and all sorts of hanging-basket plants that have become leggy with the heat. Rejuvenated, these plants will bloom again for months.

August

Replenish mulch around annual plantings. Adding another inch of pine straw or ground bark now suppresses weeds and moderates the most stressful months of the growing season.

Water container-bound plants daily and soak beds weekly, even if it rains. Use a soaker hose in the garden to ensure that the water stays in the bed. If you aren't sure how much water is reaching your plants, use a rain gauge to measure it.

Plant small chrysanthemum plants during this month.

Whiteflies can be on their tenth generation of the year by now. Long-term control relies on annual garden cleanup and removal of host plants such as privet.

Save the seeds of celosia, cosmos, four o'clock, the morning glory family (including cardinal climber and moonflower), spider flower, and zinnias. Let plants mature as much as possible before gently crushing the flower heads to collect the seeds. Separate the seeds from other materials.

September

Use a complete fertilizer on fall-blooming zinnias, marigolds, balsam *(Impatiens balsama),* celosia, and other flowers planted in July.

Get to know overwintering annuals, those flowers that perform best when planted in the fall for early spring blooms. Pansies and violas are the most familiar overwintering annuals, along with ornamental cabbage and kale, but depending on how far south you live, other possibilities include candytuft, foxglove, hollyhocks, Johnny-jump-up *(Viola tricolor),* poppies, snapdragons, and stocks.

The top transplant for this month is the garden chrysanthemum, which you should plant right away. Plants that are already in bloom or covered with flower buds will not grow much larger. For a carpet of flowers, plant chrysanthemums close together. Keep mums moist so that flowers open as they're supposed to. Deadhead first blooms so that side buds can open.

Sow seeds of the following flowers in flats for transplanting next month: calendula, candytuft, pinks, sweet alyssum, and sweet William. Grow outdoors in late-day shade in a mix of half potting soil and half compost. Keep moist; add fertilizer at half-strength every other week.

October

After five consecutive nights with temperatures in the 60s (15 to 20°C), transplant pansies, ornamental cabbage, and flowering kale. After two weeks of those temperatures, transplant the other annuals you started last month after they develop three sets of true leaves.

Sow poppy and larkspur seed with sand for better spacing. Different poppies reseed across the South; single larkspur reseeds almost everywhere.

Take a look at the newer pansy varieties to find flowers with sturdier stems, neater clumps, and more cold-hardiness.

If you feel like taking a chance on a plant in October, try sweet peas. An unseasonably cold and wet winter can do in any of your favorite annuals, but sweet peas prove especially challenging — and they're worth it. Try a tall variety on a trellis under a deciduous tree to provide winter sun and spring shade.

November

Don't mulch patches of fall-seeded annuals such as candytuft, larkspur, and poppies. Watch for seedlings and keep the beds weeded. Fertilize once before the end of the year.

As you make out your holiday wish list, consider a bottom-heat mat for starting seeds. This waterproof mat contains a thermostat that plugs into an electrical outlet and heats seed trays to optimum germination temperature. Place these mats under seeded pots, and the warmth transfers to the potting soil and quickens germination and root growth of the young plants.

December

Freezing temperatures are not always the biggest problem annuals face in winter, but wild temperature swings can be deadly to dry plants. Prevent drought damage by watering before plants wilt. For warmer water that's gentler on the plants, set timers for midday, lay your hose out in the sun, or capture rainwater in dark-colored containers before using the water to irrigate.

Sunny days bring out the caterpillars on ornamental cabbage, kale, dill, and parsley. Hand pick the varmints. If you use *Bacillus thuringiensis* (Bt), they'll still be there, but they stop feeding in about 24 hours.

Pile the mulch on transplanted annuals; make excellent, free mulch from leaves chopped up into coin-sized pieces.

Clean up your act! Rake away fallen leaves, spent flowers, and frosted plants, including weeds. Compost this debris, adding kitchen waste and the first cutting of your overseeded rye lawn. Tidying up now can mean fewer weeds, pests, and diseases next season.

Chapter 4

Month by Month in the Western States

*T*he West exhibits some of the most complex climates in the United States. In the states west of the Mississippi, annual flowers encounter some of the shortest growing seasons (in the Rocky Mountain region) and the longest (in Southern California). The Pacific Northwest has a long but cool growing season. Arizona's garden-growing season is the opposite of most other climates: Fall, winter, and spring are the seasons to enjoy annuals, because summer is too hot for them.

In this chapter, I divide the West into four subregions for growing annuals: the bulk of California, the high-altitude regions, the low-altitude deserts, and the Pacific Northwest. Each subregion has different seasons, starting times, opportunities, and challenges.

Growing Annuals in Most of California

The seasonal advice in this section works for the majority of California, with two notable exceptions:

✔ The mountains, where the growing season is much shorter: Refer to "Growing Annuals at High Altitudes."

✔ The low-elevation desert, where the main growing season for annuals is fall through early spring: See the section "Growing Annuals in Lowland Deserts."

January

Peruse mail-order catalogs or seed racks and select annual seeds for sowing soon (cool-season types) or in several months (warm-season annuals).

Start seeds of cool-season annuals indoors to set out in four to six weeks; choices include calendulas, Iceland poppies, pansies, snapdragons, and sweet peas.

Brighten your garden with already blooming annuals sold in 4-inch pots and larger sizes at garden centers. Pansies and primroses offer maximum color now — especially if they're planted in containers. Limit your planting to large annuals that are already in bloom. Save smaller-sized plants for warmer weather next month.

February

As the weather starts to warm up, and if the soil is dry enough, set out seedlings of cool-season annuals. You also can fill in empty spots in beds planted last fall. Good choices include calendulas, cinerarias, Iceland poppies, pansies, pinks, primroses, snapdragons, stocks, and violas. These plants can stand up to some frost.

This month or next, start seeds indoors of warm-season annuals, such as cosmos and lobelia. (See the April calendar in this section for more warm-season annuals.) Seeds sown around the middle of the month should be ready for transplanting by late March or early April. Wait until next month to sow seeds if you live in a cooler climate.

Sow seeds of sweet peas directly in the ground. In warm climates, make sure that you choose a heat-resistant type that's able to cope with midspring hot weather that hits at bloom time.

Sow seeds of low-growing annuals to fill in between emerging daffodils, tulips, and other spring bulbs. Good bulb covers include sweet alyssum, baby blue eyes, and wallflowers. The annuals spread and bloom while the bulbs are blooming and then help camouflage the bulb foliage as it dries up.

Fertilize cool-season annuals growing in the ground and in containers. Try to feed regularly — either monthly or twice a month.

Watch for snails and slugs around young plantings, especially if the weather is on the wet and mild side — when the population explodes. Try to eliminate insect hideouts by cleaning up piles of leaves and other garden debris. Hoe or pull out weeds fostered by winter rains before they overtake planting beds.

March

Cool-season annuals (pansies and Iceland poppies, for example) should be at their peak bloom now. Maintain top performance by monthly feeding and pinching off dead blooms. Be especially vigilant in cutting off faded pansy flowers; your goal should be to let no little seedheads form.

Except in the hottest climates, you can still plant cool-season annuals. (See the list of flowers under February in this section.)

In warmer climates, such as southern California and inland valleys, this month begins the planting time for warm-season annuals — make sure that frost danger is past and weather is heating up. (See the April calendar in this section for some suggestions on warm-season annuals.)

Prepare flower beds for major spring planting this month or next month. Improve the soil by incorporating a 2- or 3-inch layer of organic matter and complete fertilizer.

Keep watching for snails and slugs. Squish the ones you see, and set out traps for the others. (See Chapter 12.)

April

This is the main planting month for warm-season annuals: Choose from cosmos, pinks, impatiens, lobelia, marigolds, petunias, zinnias, and many others. Wait a month to plant warm-season annuals in cooler coastal climates, where you can still set out most cool-season annuals.

Soon after planting, pinch back warm-season annuals to encourage bushy growth. Impatiens, petunias, and zinnias are among many flowers that respond well to pinching.

Begin a regular fertilizer program several weeks after planting warm-season annuals. Try to feed monthly at full strength or twice monthly at half-strength.

Mulch with a layer of organic matter around young annuals to conserve moisture and curtail weeds. Continue watching for slugs and snails.

May

Plant seedlings of heat-loving annuals, including phlox, portulaca, vinca rosea, and zinnias. You also can plant the warm-season annuals recommended for April. Cosmos, marigolds, and zinnias sprout quickly if sown directly in the ground now.

Sunflowers are easy to grow from seeds sown directly in the ground. If the weather has started to warm up, plant sunflower seeds this month.

If a hot spell strikes, protect newly planted annuals with temporary shading with shade cloth or floating row covers draped over the plants.

In cool coastal climates, you can still plant cool-season annuals (pansies and violas, especially), as well as many warm-season annuals.

Continue grooming and fertilizing. Earwigs emerge as a major threat to annuals. Earwigs love dark, wet places. To create an environment that's unappealing to these pests, don't mulch between plants, cultivate the soil regularly to keep it dry, and in severe cases, spray the plants with an insecticide such as pyrethrum.

June

You still have plenty of time for major planting of warm-season annuals. Choose from the flowers given for April and May in this section. For faster results, select 4-inch pot sizes. It's a fine time to plant shady spots; warm weather encourages rapid growth of bedding begonias, coleus, impatiens, and other shade-lovers.

In all but the mildest climates, cool-season annuals are probably over the hill. Pull them out, clean up planting beds, and refresh them with a layer of organic matter dug in to a depth of 10 or 12 inches. Try to put in replacement warm-season annuals as soon as possible.

Make sure that your watering system (hose, sprinklers, or watering cans) is prepared to carry your annuals through the summer — never let your annuals dry out.

Thin seedlings of annuals sown in the ground at the spacing recommended for each flower type. Pinch back seedlings to encourage bushy growth; zinnias respond with gusto (and lots of side branching) to frequent pinching.

As weather warms, watch for signs of budworm damage (hollowed out buds and tiny black droppings) on petunias and annual geraniums *(Pelargonium).* Control this pest as described in Chapter 12.

July

This can be a surprisingly productive planting month. For quick color, look for warm-season annuals (lobelia, marigolds, petunias, and many more) in 4-inch pots or larger sizes. Transplant these flowers into pots but make sure that you add enough soil mix to encourage continued root growth; pots should have a diameter at least 2 or 3 inches larger than the nursery container.

Or start with smaller seedlings and figure that they'll last well into early fall. Best bets, especially in hotter climates, are the true heat-lovers: celosia, portulaca, salvia, vinca rosea, and zinnias. Plant in the cool of evening and provide temporary shade on hot days.

Watering is the most important chore. If you don't have a sprinkler system for beds of annuals, consider running a soaker hose through your plantings. Mulch to conserve soil moisture.

Continue to watch for budworms, which destroy blooms on geraniums and petunias. Whitish spots on petunia leaves indicate an entirely different problem: smog damage, which you can do nothing about (except, perhaps, write your congressperson).

Keep annuals going at top speed by feeding them regularly, as I explain in Chapter 9.

August

Start seeds of cool-season annuals in flats or pots to set out in late summer or early fall. The long list of possibilities includes calendulas, Iceland poppies, and pansies.

Watch for the late-summer destroyers: spider mites and white-flies. (See Chapter 12 for ways to control these pests.)

Continue to feed and pinch. If lobelia and impatiens look too lanky, cut them back by as much as a third; they'll respond with a burst of late-summer growth.

Figure out a system to water container plants, especially if you go on vacation. Container plants suffer if soil dries out and pulls away from the sides of the pots, allowing water to slip down the sides instead of soaking in. Try a small drip system attached to a faucet; you can easily add a timer.

September

The year's most productive planting season begins in many California gardens this month. Exact timing depends on where you live. In hot areas and much of southern California, wait until late in the month. Near the coast and in most of northern California, aim for midmonth.

Plant cool-season annuals now, and they'll bloom by December holidays and continue blooming through spring. Favorite cool-season choices include calendulas, Iceland poppies, pansies, primroses, snapdragons, stocks, and violas. Near the coast, you can plant some flashy annual seedlings such as cineraria, nemesia, and schizanthus, but these flowers will freeze in the parts of California that receive frost.

During hot weather, plant in the evening and provide temporary shade with shade cloth or floating row covers draped over the plants.

Extend plantings of warm-season annuals as long as you can by continuing to water thoroughly, feed, and remove faded flowers. You may want to be ruthless now: Leave summer flowers in too long, and they delay your fall planting. Pull them out when their beauty fades.

Mildew on cosmos and other summer flowers is a sign their season is over. Don't fight it. Pull out the plants.

Start seeds of cool-season annuals in flats or pots for transplanting next month. Calendulas, forget-me-nots, and Iceland poppies are the easiest to grow.

October

Sow wildflowers seeds, such as California poppy and clarkia, as well as seeds of annuals that perform like wildflowers, such as African daisy *(Dimorphotheca)*. Plant these seeds before the wet season, and let winter rains take over your watering chores.

If you plant spring-flowering bulbs, follow up with annuals on top. Pansies and violas are classic bulb covers for tulips and daffodils. Or sow seeds such as baby blue eyes, forget-me-nots, sweet alyssum, and wallflowers. Spectacular Shirley poppies can tower over wildflower-type plantings; they're easy to grow from seeds in sunny spots.

This is still a great time to plant all cool-season annuals: See the varieties listed in September in this section.

For wonderfully fragrant sweet peas as early as March, sow seeds between the middle and end of the month. Choose heat-resistant varieties if your area heats up quickly in the spring (inland southern California, for example). Before planting, soak seeds in water overnight or at least for a few hours.

Watch for snails and slugs given new life by cooling weather. If they make an appearance, deal with them as I describe in Chapter 12.

Start to regularly fertilize fall annuals two or three weeks after planting.

November

Early November is the last chance for planting cool-season annuals with expectation of midwinter flowers. You also can still plant wildflowers and bulb covers as described in October.

Snails and slugs are almost inevitable around newly planted annuals. If you don't believe it, check with a flashlight at night.

Continue regular watering until winter rains keep the soil constantly moist. Check for moisture by digging several inches into the soil.

Watch for a new crop of winter weeds brought up by watering or rainfall. Hoe or pull them while the soil is wet and soft.

December
Make sure that you keep watering if winter rains arrive late.

Plant cool-season annuals if you haven't already. You missed the warm fall weather that pushes annuals into midwinter bloom, but you still can expect a strong spring show from annuals planted now. If rains soak the soil, let it dry out a bit before planting.

Growing Annuals at High Altitudes

The high-altitude western United States — from California to Colorado, north to Montana, south to mountainous Arizona and New Mexico — offers terrific, albeit abbreviated, growing conditions for annuals. Frosts can hit late in the spring and strike early in the fall, but the cool nights and bright, dry summer weather bring out the best in many annuals. Somehow, they just look brighter in this part of the country.

If you live in a temperate, high-altitude climate (such as the mountains of the western United States and comparable climates around the world, including Switzerland, Chile, Argentina, Korea, or northern China), follow the calendar for the North, earlier in this chapter. Start seeds indoors and set out seedlings as recommended for colder sections in the northern part of the United States. Consult your local extension service, the Department of Agriculture, or the nursery for specific recommendations.

Growing Annuals in Lowland Deserts

The Southwest deserts encompass mild-winter climates of the low-elevation deserts of Arizona and California. (The mountains of Arizona and New Mexico, as well as west Texas, have a more typical cold-winter, summer-only season for growing annuals.) There's nothing else quite like the growing season of low-desert Arizona, primarily around Phoenix and Tucson, and California's Coachella Valley. Summers are hot, to say the least, and winters are sunny and warm in the day but cool at night. Glory time for annuals is late winter and early spring. This calendar starts in September to reflect the true beginning of the planting season — the low desert's "spring."

September

Get planting beds ready for the year's most rewarding planting season in the low-desert Southwest. Lay down 2 or 3 inches of organic matter, such as ground bark. Scatter complete fertilizer according to label directions and work everything in to a depth of 10 or 12 inches.

Wait until midmonth or later and set out nursery transplants for winter and spring bloom — maybe even by Christmas. Try these old reliables: calendulas, Iceland poppies, pansies, petunias, snapdragons, stocks, and violas. Provide temporary shade during the hottest weather.

Early in the month, you still have time to start annual flower seeds in flats or pots to transplant into the ground later in the fall. Calendulas and Iceland poppies are easy to start from seed.

If summer annuals are still going strong, keep them watered thoroughly and fertilize monthly or every two weeks.

October

Continue to set out annuals for blooms before the end of the year. (See the list for September in this section.) Water thoroughly after planting and provide temporary shade during extra-hot spells.

Sow seeds of low-spreading annuals to cover bare spots in bulb beds. If your timing is good, everything will bloom all at once. Terrific bulb covers include baby blue eyes, forget-me-nots, and white sweet alyssum. You can also sow wildflower seeds directly in the ground for a big spring show; try California poppy and African daisy.

Start regular feeding a few weeks after planting annuals.

November

There's still time to plant for winter and spring bloom. Top choices for sunny spots are ageratum, calendula, candytuft, clarkia, larkspur, lobelia, petunia, snapdragon, stock, and sweet pea. For shady spots, plant pinks, pansies, primroses, and violas.

This month is the best time of year to sow wildflower seeds, including California poppies and many others. Make sure that the planting area receives full sun all winter.

Cooler weather encourages a new crop of aphids, plus slugs and snails. For information on controlling these pests, see Chapter 12.

December

Where else can you set out annuals over the holidays? You still have time to plant seedlings of calendulas, Iceland poppies, and all the rest.

Watch your soil for signs of dryness, and water as needed.

January

After the holidays, nurseries stock up with blooming annuals in small pots. Shop for color that you can use right away in pots or in gaps in planting beds.

Watch for aphids and take steps to control them.

Winter rains and cool temperatures bring up seasonal weeds, which you can pull or hoe. Or mulch beds with a layer of organic matter to smother weeds and weed seeds.

February

Cool-season annuals — pansies, snapdragons, stocks, and the rest — are peaking this month in the low desert. Maintain top performance by removing dead flowers, watering thoroughly, and feeding regularly.

Indoors, you can start seeds of warm-season annuals (marigold, salvia, and many more) to transplant into the garden in four to six weeks.

Prepare beds for spring planting — as long as plants growing in them have finished their season.

March

In the low desert, transplant warm-season annuals, such as celosia, marigolds, portulaca, and salvia. Pinch back at planting time and snip off flowers to encourage bushier growth.

A few weeks after planting, fertilize young annuals and begin a regular schedule of fertilizing (monthly or twice monthly).

April

Plant heat-loving annuals, such as cosmos, marigolds, and zinnias.

Adjust the frequency of sprinkler systems as the weather heats up. If your annuals aren't on a sprinkler system, consider a soaker hose. (Put it on a timer, if you want.)

May

Spring flowers are winding down. Pull them out and replace them with heat-lovers.

Pinch tips of young annuals for bushier growth, especially marigolds and zinnias.

June

This is your last chance to plant for summer blooms. Make sure that you choose from among the true heat-lovers: globe amaranth, salvia, and the most reliable of all, vinca rosea.

July and August

Water and mulch. Water and mulch. You don't do any planting at this time of year.

Feed summer annuals regularly. Remove faded flowers.

Growing Annuals in the Pacific Northwest

Compared with California, the Pacific Northwest, including the milder parts of British Columbia, has a much more straightforward pattern for growing annuals — a long season from spring through fall. West of the Cascade Range, the lingering cool spring tends to favor cool-season annuals, and the relatively cool summers encourage spectacular displays of annuals, such as the legendary Butchart Gardens in Victoria, British Columbia, and magnificent public gardens in Seattle, Washington, and Portland, Oregon. East of the Cascades, where winters are longer and much colder, the annual season is shorter, but the heat and the dry climate are terrific for sun-loving annuals.

January

Study catalogs and order seeds for starting indoors in a few weeks or outdoors in a few months. Prepare an indoor area for starting seeds.

February

Start seeds of annuals indoors for transplanting in spring. Best bets include ageratum, calendulas, California poppies, cosmos, gloriosa daisies, nicotiana, pansies, Shirley poppies, and snapdragons.

If the ground isn't too wet, you can start seeding the following hardy annuals directly in the ground late this month: calendula, clarkia, cornflower, dwarf pink, English daisy *(Bellis perennis),* pansy, stock, and sweet alyssum. Optimistic gardeners traditionally sow sweet peas on Washington's Birthday.

Try transplanting hardy annuals, such as pansies and primroses, if nurseries offer them and the soil is dry enough to be dug. Or plant them in containers.

March

Prepare beds for major spring planting as long as the soil isn't too wet. Dig 10 to 12 inches deep and add 2 or 3 inches of organic matter. Blend in thoroughly, along with complete fertilizer.

Sow sweet peas seeds before midmonth; to improve sprouting success, soak seeds in water overnight or at least for a few hours. Also sow seeds of other hardy annuals listed in February in this section.

Continue indoor seeding of annuals listed in February. Begin sowing warm-season annuals, such as marigolds and zinnias, for transplanting when the weather warms up in May.

April

Set out transplants of cool-season annuals, such as calendulas, pansies, and snapdragons. Begin transplanting warm-season annuals if the weather and soil have warmed up.

Watch for snails and slugs to begin their most damaging season around young annuals.

May

This is the Northwest's prime time for planting annuals. Almost anything will grow if planted now, including transplants of bedding begonias, celosia, cosmos, geraniums (*Pelargonium*), impatiens, lobelia, marigolds, nicotiana, love-in-a-mist, petunias, salvia, snapdragons, sunflowers, sweet alyssum, and verbena.

Start feeding annuals two or three weeks after planting. (Chapter 9 explains the types and uses of fertilizer.)

Protect young annuals from snails and slugs.

Sow asters, cosmos, marigolds, and zinnias from seed directly in the ground.

June

Planting season continues, but try to finish soon to get the longest season. See the list of choices for May.

Continue to sow seeds of heat-loving annuals, such as marigolds and zinnias.

Soon after planting annuals, pinch them back to encourage bushy growth: Impatiens, petunias, snapdragons, and zinnias are among many flowers that respond well to pinching.

Continue regular feeding and grooming.

July

Keep annuals going strong by feeding them regularly.

If planting beds need extra watering, run a soaker hose between the plants.

You can still plant annual seeds for later summer bloom. Cosmos is an excellent, reliable late-bloomer.

August

Watch for late-summer invaders, such as spider mites. Treat them according to the instructions in Chapter 12.

If impatiens and lobelia get a bit straggly, cut them back by about a third to encourage a late-summer burst of growth.

September

Extend the summer bloom season by removing dead flowers and watering as needed.

For color until frost strikes, set out dwarf pinks, Johnny-jump-ups, pansies, stocks, and kale.

October

Remove over-the-hill summer annuals. Clean up beds and turn over the soil for fall or spring planting.

Keep hardy annuals, such as pansies, going for another few weeks by continuing to feed, water, and groom them.

Sow wildflowers and other annuals that get off to an early start in spring, including calendula, California poppy, candytuft, larkspur, and linaria. Before planting, clear the area of weeds and rake lightly. Scatter the seeds, cover them with a thin layer of organic matter, and then water thoroughly.

November

You still have time to sow seeds of hardy annuals and wildflowers for blooms next spring: See the list in October in this section.

Clean up all annual planting beds.

Chapter 5

The Big Eight: Popular, Reliable Annuals

In This Chapter

▶ Introducing eight darlings of the annuals world

▶ Choosing fail-proof annuals for your garden

▶ Understanding when and how to plant each annual

*T*his chapter gets you started with what I consider to be the Big Eight, a somewhat arbitrary grouping that, nonetheless, represents some of the most popular and reliable annuals currently available. These plants are where the most plant breeding action has occurred, where you find the most new varieties, and where you encounter the most bewildering array of selections at the nursery or in the seed catalogs.

To be included here, an annual has to do at least a couple things:

✓ It has to be worth growing without a whole lot of trouble. Remember, though, that it may not perform equally well in all climates and garden situations.

✓ It has to be available through normal channels, either as seedlings at major nurseries and garden centers or as seeds sold by big-time mail-order catalogs or on nursery seed racks.

The sections in this chapter don't tell you everything there is to know about each plant, just the important stuff that you need to consider to choose your annuals and grow them successfully. I mention flower size and typical colors, blooming season, size of plants, and how to use the plants in your garden.

Bedding begonia, or wax begonia (Begonia semperflorens)

Crisp, glossy, and succulent, bedding begonias look good enough to eat. The plant's flowers, which last from late spring through summer, are small but profuse, in shades of pink, red, and white. Begonia leaves can be colorful, too, with dark bronzy tones and bright greens. The plants grow 6 to 12 inches tall. Use them to edge borders, as mass plantings in beds, or in containers.

Set out transplants in full sun in mild-summer climates, or in part shade in hot-summer climates. Plant in spring, after the danger of frost has passed. Space dwarf plants 8 inches apart and taller varieties 12 inches apart.

Bedding begonias are easy to grow and very dependable. You can help them along by improving the soil with plenty of organic matter and keeping the soil moist. In hot climates, bedding begonias need shade from hottest sun.

Geraniums (Pelargonium)

Some of my most vivid, endearing impressions of annuals involve geraniums: a window box full of bright red geraniums lighting up the stony visage of the only bank in a Swiss village; ground-cover geraniums crawling in and out of the purple bougainvillea on a Laguna Beach hillside as lush and tangled as a Cambodian jungle; the clay pots, unwatered for weeks, outside my dry cleaner's front door, leaves coated with way-ward cat hair but bravely hoisting two or three orange flowers.

The annual flower that most people call a geranium is, botanically speaking, a *Pelargonium*. This information is important to know because a very different plant uses *Geranium* as its botanical name. Look for the word *Pelargonium* to be sure that the plant you're buying is the annual described here, and chalk the whole mess up to another case where botanical names create more confusion than they clear up.

Geraniums flourish worldwide and are universal favorites because they're easy to grow and always seem to muster up a bright, crisp look. They're great for beginners — or just about anyone. Geraniums actually have increased in popularity now that so many new varieties are grown from seeds. (Formerly, most geraniums were propagated from cuttings.)

Geraniums are actually perennials and can survive for years in mild climates. In southern California, some people refer to them as "rats of the garden" for their persistence. In cold climates, you can move plants indoors to a sunny spot and keep them through the winter.

Geraniums are usually sold as annuals in pots of various sizes, from 3 inches on up, often in bloom already. Here are the three main types you can find:

✔ **Zonal geraniums** *(Pelargonium hortorum):* These are the most familiar, with flower clusters standing tall above deep green, velvety-soft leaves. Colors include white, orange, red, pink, rose, and violet. Some have fancy leaves that are splashed, spotted, and bordered with darker colors. Plants can grow up to 3 feet tall, but usually reach 12 to 18 inches in one season. For a mass planting, space plants 12 inches apart. These are classics for containers of all sizes.

Dozens of varieties are available. Among the strains to check out are Multibloom and Orbit. The Multibloom Strain comes in eight colors, has numerous bloom stems, flowers early, and grows 10 to 12 inches tall. The Orbit Strain grows about the same size, has compact plants, and produces flowers in a dozen and a half colors.

✔ **Ivy geraniums** *(Pelargonium peltatum):* These plants seem made for hanging baskets or to cover ground. Branches stretch out like ivy, up to 2 or 3 feet. Foliage is glossy and smooth; flower colors include lavender, pink, red, and white. Look for varieties developed specifically for hanging baskets: Summer Showers, a winner of the European Fleuroselect award, is very pendulous and comes in five colors. Breakaway Hybrid, in red or salmon, has 5- or 6-inch flower heads and bushy spreading growth.

✔ **Scented geraniums** *(Pelargonium):* Crush the foliage to get a sniff of apples, mint, roses, lime, and many other scents that are gentle on the nose. The foliage carries the fragrance. Flowers are small — not the reason you

choose to grow scented geraniums. Plants grow 12 to
36 inches tall. Use them in borders, pots, hanging baskets,
or in an herb garden. Be sure to grow them where you
can appreciate their fragrance at close range. There are
countless types; choose the ones that smell best to you.

Set out geraniums in the spring. Provide full sun or part shade
in hot climates. Try to plant in soil with fast drainage.
Geraniums are very responsive to pinching. For bushy growth,
pinch out tips of young growth to force side branching.
Remove dead flowers.

What are some of the problems that plague geraniums?
Budworm is most notorious. It hollows out flowers and can
wipe out the bloom season. Look for telltale tiny black droppings in the vicinity of the flowers. Control as described in
Chapter 12. Also watch for aphids, spider mites, and whiteflies.

Impatiens

Don't worry if garden snobs look down their noses at impatiens. Every year, I try a few new things by the back fence, but
nothing has ever come close to competing with impatiens.
Not only do they survive the denizens of the deep shade
(snails and who knows what other mysterious creatures lurk
there), but they also bloom heavily from early summer to
Thanksgiving without a ray of direct sunlight.

Impatiens are easy to grow, bloom better than just about anything else in shady conditions, hardly ever run into problems,
stay compact, and have attractive foliage. No wonder they're
best-selling annuals in all regions. You can use impatiens for
mass plantings under trees, for edging shady borders, or
mixed in with ferns or other shade-lovers. They're also great
in baskets or containers — try to choose varieties with pendulous stems developed for this purpose.

You can grow impatiens from seeds or cuttings, but nursery
transplants are the easiest. Here are the main types:

✔ The standard impatiens *(Impatiens walleriana),* sometimes called busy lizzie because of the way that the seed
pods pop open, comes in many strains and varieties. The
flowers are usually about 1 to 2 inches wide and come in

colors may be too basic for some people; if a flower can be condemned for being too orange, marigolds deserve at least a 15-yard penalty.

The marigold, like the petunia, has been the subject of decades of plant breeding. As a result, we are blessed with some great plants but a bewildering number of choices. It pays to become a bit familiar with flower forms and plant growth habits.

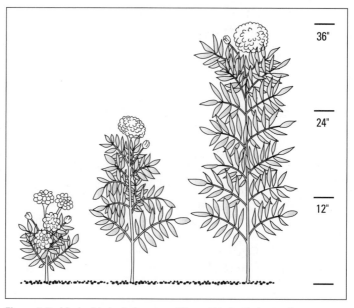

Figure 5-2: Marigolds include many different kinds of plants. Some are low with delicate orange flowers. Others are tall with softball-size flowers.

- ✔ **African marigolds *(Tagetes erecta):*** These plants, also called American marigolds, are the towering types — up to 36 inches tall, with huge flowers up to 5 inches across and so thickly double-petaled that they look like round balls. Use them in the background or at the back of borders. Lady Hybrid comes in deep orange, creamy yellow, gold, and other shades. The classic, clear yellow 'First Lady' is an All-America winner, with sturdy plants reaching 20 inches tall. Climax is even taller, up to 36 inches, and has bigger flowers in a range of colors. White marigolds, unknown until recent decades, are now available in several varieties such as 'French Vanilla'. Another white marigold, 'Snowdrift', grows 2 feet tall and is valued for its ability to tolerate afternoon shade.

✔ **French marigolds *(Tagetes patula)*:** These plants are much more compact (6 to 12 inches tall) and have single or double, smaller flowers (1 to 2 inches) in great abundance — some varieties have red shades. Also look for striking bicolors, combining yellow and maroon, for instance. Use these for edging borders, mass plantings, and in containers. There are dozens and dozens of kinds: The Aurora Series blooms early, with 2½-inch double flowers on rounded 12-inch plants. 'Naughty Marietta', 10 inches tall, has single flowers that boldly combine golden yellow and maroon.

✔ **Triploid hybrids:** These hybrids are the result of crossing African and French marigolds. They boast numerous 3-inch flowers on compact plants up to a foot tall. One neat thing about these hybrids is that they don't produce seeds, which means that you don't have to bother cutting off dead flowers to sustain the bloom. Look for the outstanding Nugget Supreme Series.

✔ **Signet marigolds *(Tagetes tenuifolia)*:** Here is where the word "dainty" enters the marigold lexicon — these dwarf plants are bushy with colorful masses of little flowers only an inch across. Use signets as a border edging or in containers. 'Gem', about 12 inches tall, includes gold, lemon, and orange flowers.

Plant marigolds in the spring after frost danger, when the weather warms up. Nurseries offer dozens of varieties as transplants. Marigolds are as easy as any plant to sow directly in the ground — a perfect opportunity for first-time gardeners in areas with long growing seasons. Choose a sunny spot. Prepare the soil as described in Chapter 6. Broadcast seeds and cover with about ¼ inch of soil and keep moist. Seeds usually sprout in a few days if the soil is warm, and plants begin flowering in about 6 to 8 weeks. Thin seedlings so that they stand from 6 inches apart (dwarfs) up to 24 inches apart (biggest, tallest types).

Removing dead flowers greatly prolongs the bloom season and improves the appearance of the plant — it's easier to do, of course, with the big-flowered type than with the prolific bloomers. Marigolds attract no special pests, but watch for slugs and snails when plants are young.

Pansies and Violas (Viola wittrockiana)

The familiar faces of pansies and violas come out to greet us like old friends early each spring. Tolerant of cold, they can stand a light snow cover and are among the first annuals to bloom. In mild climates, they can flower through winter. For generations, pansies and violas have brightened the California racetracks when it's too cold for thoroughbreds and annuals anywhere else.

Technically, pansies are just big violas, having 2- to 4-inch flowers that come in a range of bright colors: blue, purple, rose, yellow, and white, often striped or dramatically blotched. Majestic Giant Strain has 4-inch flowers with big blotches. 'Maxim Marina', an All-America winner, combines light and dark blue and is resistant to heat and cold. Plants grow up to 8 inches tall. Use them in mass plantings, in borders, mixed in with bulbs, in containers, and as an edging.

Violas stay less than 6 or 8 inches tall. Colors are mostly solid, including blue, apricot, red, purple, white, red, and yellow. Johnny-jump-up *(viola tricolor)* looks like a miniature pansy with purple and yellow flowers. It stays low and fits right in nestled among spring bulbs, such as daffodils.

In cold-winter climates, plant pansies and violas in early spring, several weeks before the last frost. In mild-winter climates, plant in the fall or late winter. Check locally to see when to plant pansies in your area. More and more cold-climate gardeners are planting pansies in the fall for a bit of fall color; they are proving to survive through the winter under a light snow and start off strong in the spring.

Set out transplants in full sun or part shade. (Full sun is vital for winter bloom.) Improve the soil by adding plenty of organic matter. Space plants 6 inches apart. Feel free to cut flowers for indoor use — the plants appreciate the effort. Remove all dead flowers. Hot weather tends to end things for pansies and violas; when growth looks shabby, pull them out.

Petunias

What's simpler than a petunia — easily recognizable and pretty easy to grow? Not to make a big deal out of nothing, but what *isn't* so simple is figuring out which kinds of petunia to plant. Allow me to guide you down the baffling rows of the nursery or through the pages of the seed catalog.

The petunia breeding industry spans more than a hundred years. The state-of-the-art petunias you see today are the result of hybridization; they're specially bred for increased vigor and predictability. Modern petunia colors include yellow as well as deep purple, in addition to the traditional pink, red, white, light blue, and bicolors. The blooms can be imaginatively ruffled and frilled, but the typical funnel-shaped, single flower is still the most popular type.

Today's petunias retain one important old-fashioned virtue: a long bloom season, from summer until frost. In the hottest climates of the Southwest and Southeast, summer is too hot; but in some of those climates with mild winters, such as Arizona, petunias can be planted in fall for winter and spring bloom.

Petunias come in single and double blooms and a variety of classes, as shown in Figure 5-3. Pay attention to the two main petunia classes:

- ✔ **Grandifloras:** These boast the biggest flowers, usually up to 4½ inches wide, in single or ruffled forms. Plants grow up to 24 inches tall and 24 to 36 inches wide — sometimes on the rangy side. Cascade and Supercascade Strains are well-deserved favorites for hanging baskets and containers, where they can spill over the sides. 'Fluffy Ruffles' has frilly, double flowers up to 6 inches wide; plants grow to 18 inches. Look for the 1998 All-America Selection winner, 'Prism Sunshine', with a lovely, large 3-inch-wide bloom.

- ✔ **Multifloras:** Compared to grandifloras, the plants are more compact and the flowers are smaller (about 2 inches wide) but more abundant, either single or double. This is the type of petunia you see used by the acre in public gardens — very colorful and very reliable. Look for Ultra Series, 12-inch compact plants, with large, single flowers in more than a dozen colors. Double Delight

Series has full double flowers. 'Summer Sun', the original yellow petunia, is still a striking winner.

You may also encounter millifloras, a newer type, with small flowers (about 1½ inches wide) and a dwarf habit of growth that's ideal for pots, baskets, and border edging. Fantasy, a 10-inch dwarf in mixed colors, is outstanding.

'Purple Wave', an All-America winner, can rightfully be called a ground-cover petunia, spreading up to 4 feet while growing no more than 6 inches tall. A pink variety is also available. Also look for outstanding new trailing strains, excellent in hanging baskets or as ground covers: Supertunia Strain is fast growing and available in eight colors; Surfinia Strain comes in shades of blue, purple, and pink, as well as white.

Growing petunias from the tiny seeds is very tricky. It's simplest to start with nursery transplants. Set them out in full sun in spring after frost danger. Space plants 8 to 12 inches apart, depending on variety — new ground-cover types can be spaced farther apart. Soon after planting, begin pinching back tips to encourage bushier growth. Be sure to remove dead flowers. Late in the season, when growth becomes leggy, cut back plants by as much as a half to force a new spurt of growth.

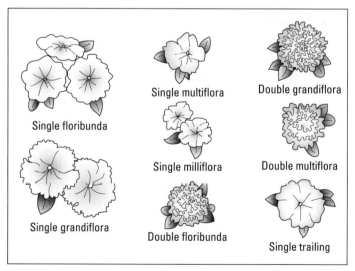

Single floribunda

Single multiflora

Double grandiflora

Single milliflora

Double multiflora

Single grandiflora

Double floribunda

Single trailing

Figure 5-3: With single and double blooms; multiflora, grandiflora, and milliflora classes; and more, petunias are a diverse bunch.

Petunia problems are rare, but watch for tobacco budworms, which devour flowers and leaves. Smog has been a 50-year nemesis to petunias; petunia leaves become splotched during bad-air episodes. You can't do much about smog, but you can be aware of the conditions in your area and choose varieties listed as smog-resistant if pollution is a problem where you live. Also watch for the usual offenders, including aphids, snails, and slugs.

Vinca rosea, or Madagascar periwinkle (Catharanthus roseus)

This is the champion of hot-climate performers, thriving in desert climates such as the southwestern United States and northern Mexico. Even in midsummer, an abundance of 1½-inch white or pink flowers looks crisp and fresh, and the foliage manages to stay shiny and deep green. Plants grow up to 20 inches tall; compact varieties reach half that size or less.

Use vinca rosea to edge a border, as a low-growing mass planting, or spilling from a container. Choose from many new and improved varieties. 'Apricot Delight' is outstanding; it grows 10 or 12 inches tall and has an extra-long bloom season.

Vinca rosea is an easy plant to grow. Set out transplants in full sun in spring, when warm weather has arrived and the danger of frost has passed. Space plants 8 to 12 inches apart. For vigorous and lush growth, make sure that you provide plenty of water — as long as soil drains quickly. Bloom season can extend until the first frost, or later in mild climates.

Zinnias (Zinnia elegans)

Easy to grow, sun-loving, and long-blooming, zinnias always rank near the top among summer annuals. The colors seem right for the season — red, yellow, orange, purple, white, salmon, pink, and rose. There's even a green variety called 'Envy'.

Zinnias come in several flower forms, two of which you owe it to yourself to consider:

- ✔ *Cactus* refers to large, double blooms with quilled, pointed petals.

- ✔ *Dahlia-flowered* types are similar but have flat, rounded petals.

Dwarf types, from 6 to 12 inches, work well as border edgings, in containers, or massed in low plantings. The Peter Pan series grows about a foot tall and has 3-inch flowers in cream, plum, scarlet, white, gold, orange, and pink. 'Small World Cherry' is an All-America winner, with dark red blooms on 14-inch plants — great for beds and cutting.

Taller types do well at the back of a border or massed in beds. 'Ruffles', about 30 inches tall, with 3 to 3½-inch flowers, is excellent for cutting. For a striking midsummer bouquet, try 'Ruffles Cherry'. Also look for bicolor types in candy-cane colors; 'Peppermint Stick' grows about 24 inches tall.

For humid climates or wherever mildew is a problem, your best bet is 'Pinwheel', a compact and bushy zinnia that grows to 12 inches tall and has 3½-inch daisylike flowers. Another zinnia known for its resistance to powdery mildew is Oklahoma Mix, a new mix that grows 2 feet tall and has 1½ inch flowers. (Read more about powdery mildew in Chapter 12.)

A relative of *Zinnia elegans, Zinnia angustifolia* is a perennial in mild climates that acts more or less as a 15- or 18-inch ground cover with bright 1-inch flowers. The Star Series is outstanding, with dainty, star-shaped flowers in gold, orange, or white — a great choice for containers or mass plantings.

Plant zinnias in your sunniest spot, preferably in well-drained soil. Wait to plant until late spring, well after frost danger, when the soil and air are definitely warm. Nursery transplants are widely sold but are on the touchy side; be careful not to disturb roots and don't buy overgrown seedlings. Zinnias are so easy to grow from seeds that sowing directly in the ground usually works best. Thin dwarf plants to stand 6 inches apart; thin taller varieties to 12 inches apart.

Pinching the tips of young plants encourages them to develop bushiness; zinnias are highly responsive to pinching. Cut off faded flowers to encourage a long season of blooms.

 Zinnias are mildew prone, especially in foggy or humid climates. Reduce the likelihood of mildew by watering them with a ground-level irrigation system rather than overhead sprinklers. Also be on the lookout for snails and slugs. If you spot any, run straight to Chapter 12 for help.

Chapter 6

Preparing the Soil

● ●

In This Chapter

▶ Improving the earth

▶ Determining the type of soil in your yard

▶ Adding goodies to the soil

▶ Calculating your soil's pH

▶ Dealing with drainage

▶ Digging your flower bed

● ●

"**D**ig a ten-dollar hole for a ten-cent plant." That old gardening expression is a great way to look at soil preparation for annual flowers. You can spend loads of money on fine geraniums or the newest petunias, but they'll grow like ragamuffins if the soil is shabby. The opposite is also true: Plain-Jane annuals can blossom into real knockouts if you grow them in truly superior soil.

For living proof, conduct the following experiment. Pamper a salvia plant by growing it in a hole filled with high-quality potting soil and fertilizer, and plant another salvia in a quickly dug hole without potting soil or fertilizer. The salvia grown in the good soil will be taller and bushier and will produce a double quota of flowers. Annuals this healthy make you feel happy every time you look at them.

Taking Stock of What You Have

Improving your soil depends on what type of soil you find when you start digging. Based on the size of its particles, soil falls into three basic categories: loam, clay, and sand. See Figure 6-1 for a visual comparison of the three types.

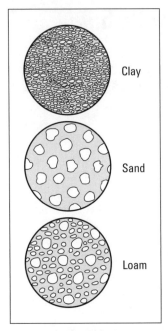

Clay

Sand

Loam

Figure 6-1: Most likely, your soil type is clay, sand, or loam.

Loam is where the heart is

If your shovel turns up loose, crumbly mounds of earth that fall apart like moist chocolate cake, count yourself lucky. This dreamy type of soil is called *loam,* and it's what everybody else wishes for. Loam is made up of soil particles that are larger than clay particles, but smaller than grains of sand. Loam also may have small rocks and quite a bit of *organic matter* — the material left behind when leaves, plants, and other living things decay. Organic matter gives any soil a slightly spongy character, which helps it hold moisture well and which is wonderfully hospitable to delicate plant roots.

Some people are lucky and have gardens composed of mostly loam soil. If you're one of them, you can skip ahead to the next chapter. But if your soil is coarser or finer than loam, read on. This chapter's for you.

Can you come out and clay?

Clay soils are over-endowed with extremely fine soil particles. In fact, the particles are so fine that they pack together very tightly, making it hard for roots to penetrate and excluding the air and water that roots need to grow. Technically, any soil composed of more than 35 percent clay particles is a clay soil. But you don't need to take your soil to a laboratory; you know you have clay soil if it feels squishy in your hands when it's wet, or if it sticks to your shovel or to the bottom of your shoes.

Gardeners sometimes complain about clay because it dries out slowly, but souped-up, reconditioned clay (that is, clay that's been amended with plenty of organic matter) is great for flowers. Clay soil holds water and nutrients for a long time, because tiny clay particles stick together with very little breathing space between them. Add organic matter to expand the spaces between particles and to help your clay soil hold air, and you have a highly drought-tolerant soil that should serve you very well.

The nitty gritty on sand

Sandy soil is pretty obvious. It dries out quickly after it rains, and you can build dirty sand castles with it when it's wet. Rub it between your fingers, and it feels gritty and coarse.

If you live in a high-rainfall area, sandy soil is good. Excess rain filters through sand quickly, and that's better than having the water puddling up around plant roots. As the rainwater flows through your flower bed and down to the groundwater below, so do plant nutrients. The same cure that helps clay soil — adding organic matter — also benefits sandy soil by helping it do a better job of holding onto water and nutrients. Mulches that stop moisture from evaporating from the soil's surface also are a big boon when your soil type is sand.

Building Better Soil

A few places on earth boast soil that is naturally dark, deep, and cushiony and weeds that bend to your will like well-trained dogs. Chances are good that these places are not in your yard — and they're definitely not in mine, either. Instead, you may have one little spot that's not riddled with tree roots or covered with concrete (although it may feel like concrete when you try to stick a shovel in it). Or maybe you moved into a new house whose yard has no topsoil.

The underground status of your chosen site can have any number of problems, but fortunately, you can take steps to make the soil better. And if you really want to, you can always abandon the idea of digging a proper in-ground bed and, instead, grow your annuals in containers or raised beds that you fill with exactly the kind of soil you want.

Giving your soil some breathing room

One of the main deficiencies in soil is free: air! You can add air by cultivating the soil, something that's easy to say but hard to do, unless you have a rotary tiller. *Cultivating* is the process of turning over and breaking up the soil — with a shovel, digging fork, or rotary tiller — and then chopping at it with a rake or pronged hoe until the big clods of dirt break into little clods. The next step is gathering up the weeds, rocks, and tree roots that your digging turned up. Finally, you repeat the whole process.

The purpose of all this work is to open up billions and billions of tiny air pockets in the soil. If you don't squeeze the air out again by walking over the bed, these air pockets become little holding tanks for soil moisture and also make cushy surroundings for plant roots.

You can get a lot more air into the soil if you cultivate it when it's reasonably dry. (See the section "Making the Bed" later in this chapter.) Wet soil tends to stick together in globs, and the globs get harder and stickier the more you try to dig. Mixing organic matter, fertilizer, and other soil amendments into very wet soil is almost impossible. Wait until the soil dries a bit.

If your soil tends to be wet and clammy in the spring when you're ready to plant annual flowers, you can avoid the frustration of working with wet soil by preparing your beds in the fall, when dry conditions often prevail. Doing the heavy-lifting of soil preparation in the fall means all the amendments have plenty of time to work their way into the minute recesses of the soil. Come spring, all you need do is a bit of cleanup and you're ready to plant.

Going organic

Transforming plain soil into premium-quality stuff that supports spectacular annuals is usually a simple matter of adding organic matter and fertilizer as you dig and cultivate your bed.

Garden centers sell a wide range of products that qualify as *organic matter* — a substance that is, or was, alive. For example, anything labeled as 100 percent compost is usually a good bet. Many organic amendments are by-products of the forestry industry, such as wood chips and bark. When you buy wood by-products, look for the words "nitrified" and "composted" on the bag. These are your clues that the contents are ready to go to work in your soil by delivering their many benefits.

Compost

When different kinds of dead plant material are piled together, dampened, and stirred or turned every week or so to keep air in the mixture, they become *compost* after a month (or two or three). Products labeled as compost can be made from all sorts of stuff, but they usually are created by enterprising people who have tapped into nature's wastebasket. Fallen leaves, shredded Christmas trees, and wood chips left from tree trimming crews often find their way to compost manufacturing facilities. Sawdust from lumber mills, peanut hulls from peanut processing plants, and hundreds of other agricultural by-products also are turned into compost.

Unfortunately, you don't know exactly what you are getting in commercial compost unless you open a bag and feel around in there with your hands. You can expect to find little bits of sticks and other recognizable things in a bag of compost, but judge quality mainly by the texture of the material, which should be soft and springy. If you plan to buy big quantities of compost, compare products packaged by different companies to find the best texture. A 3-inch layer of packaged compost, worked into the soil, is a liberal helping that should give instant results. To estimate how much you need, figure that a

40-pound bag (that may actually weigh more or less than that weight, depending on how it's been stored) covers a square yard of bed space.

Composting your yard trimmings and kitchen scraps is economical because you get for free something you would otherwise have to purchase. It's also environmentally friendly, because it keeps your leftovers out of landfills. Many people, including those working at your local nursery, can get you started making compost. Or check out *Gardening For Dummies,* by Michael MacCaskey and the Editors of the National Gardening Association. It has a whole chapter about composting.

Composted manure

Rotted manure doesn't sound as good as composted manure, does it? But they both mean the same thing — the stuff that you find in bags labeled *manure.* Composting is almost always necessary to deodorize manure, so you need not worry about stinking up your yard by using packaged manure products.

In addition to conditioning soil by improving its texture, composted manure usually contains respectable amounts of nitrogen and other important plant nutrients. The percentage of nutrients varies with the type of manure.

The amount of manure to use depends on the type of manure and your soil type. Sandy soil can use twice as much manure as clay, but you don't want to overdose either way. With bulky manure from large animals (cows, horses, goats, sheep, and elephants), start with a 1-inch layer, or about 40 pounds per 3 square yards. Follow package application rates when using stronger manure, such as that from rabbits, chickens, and birds.

Humus

Bags labeled *humus* are the wild cards of the soil amendment world. Anything that qualifies as organic matter for soil, or any soil/organic-matter mixture, can be considered humus. Unlike compost, which is supposed to be cultured under controlled conditions, humus comes from more humble beginnings. For example, it may be 2-year-old sawdust and wood chips from a lumber mill mixed with rotten leaves and dark topsoil. Or it may be rotten hay mixed with soil and sand. You just don't know what you'll get until you buy a bag and open it up. If the humus has a loose, spongy texture and dark color, and you like the way it feels and smells, go for it. For a 2- to 3-inch layer, 40 pounds per 2 square yards is a good rough estimate of the quantity to use.

Topsoil

Breaking into bags of topsoil to see what's inside is always interesting. Sometimes, the content is exactly what you may find in bags of humus or compost, and other times it may look more like unbelievably black soil. Topsoil is almost always cheap. You can use bagged topsoil as a soil amendment, or you can use so much of it that your flower bed is filled with mostly imported topsoil and only a little of the native stuff.

If your soil basically disgusts you, bring home several bags of topsoil, along with humus, manure, and compost. Use the topsoil as the main ingredient for your witch's brew of new soil. Of course, if you want to use primarily topsoil, you must either plant a raised bed or dig out the soil you don't like and dump it somewhere else.

Peat moss

Peat moss is a very spongy brown material taken from peat bogs in Canada, Michigan, and a few other places. The popularity of peat moss, an old standby, has passed its peak now that so many folks have become concerned that gardeners are using up peat moss much faster than Mother Nature can make it.

Peat moss is superb at absorbing and holding huge amounts of water, while frustrating soilborne fungi that can cause plant diseases. Unfortunately, peat bogs take about a thousand years to regenerate after they are harvested. Because of this environmental concern, you may want to limit your use of peat moss to situations where it's most valuable, such as creating special soil mixtures for container-grown plants or for planting shrubs that really love it, such as azaleas and rhododendrons.

Checking your soil's pH

When you're out buying fertilizer, you may as well tap into the local expertise to see whether you also need some lime. *Lime* is finely ground limestone, and it's used to raise the pH (acidity or alkalinity) of naturally acidic soil to make it "near neutral."

Plants don't like strongly acidic soil because it hampers their ability to take up nutrients and feed themselves. Many soils in areas that were heavily wooded before civilization moved in are naturally acidic. If a nursery professional tells you that everybody in your area has acidic soil that needs added lime, you should do it, too. But if you suspect that people who know more about bubble gum than soil are staffing your garden center, you can buy a simple pH test kit and check your soil yourself. This test takes less than five minutes and is sort of fun.

If you live in the southwestern United States, you may find out that adding lime is the worst thing you can do for your soil, because you live in an area where the soil pH tends to be alkaline (a high pH rather than a low one). Strongly alkaline soil is difficult for plants, too, and can be corrected by adding small amounts of garden sulfur to the soil or by mixing in acidic soil amendments, such as composted leaves, rotted sawdust, or peat moss. If you go the sulfur route, buy only a little. About 2 pounds is all you should need to lower the pH in 50 square feet of soil.

For growing annuals, your pH doesn't need to be exactly on target, but it shouldn't be extreme, either. Soil pH is rated numerically on a scale from 0 to 14. Most annuals grow just fine if the pH is between 5.8 and 7.5. Absolute neutral is 7.0.

Dealing with Delinquent Drainage

If you go to dig your flower bed and find that the soil there is damp and swampy even though the rest of the yard seems dry, you may have a drainage problem. Think back to the last time you witnessed a heavy rain. Did that spot still have a puddle several hours later? If so, the verdict has to be *delinquent drainage,* which means that the soil holds too much water for too long a time.

Sometimes, you can correct a drainage problem by aerating the soil and adding organic matter, but drainage problems usually are caused by factors other than poor-quality soil. For example, an underground spring or other moving water may be beneath the spot, or maybe it's the lowest elevation around, so rainwater is always going to pool up there.

Whatever the cause, you probably should look elsewhere for a place to grow flowers. Bad drainage means that the roots of any plants that do grow there are deprived of air and exposed to excessive amounts of water, instead. Because very few annual flowers are willing to put up with this kind of abuse, they develop root rot in wet soils. One notable exception you might try if you have wet soil is the cardinal flower *(Lobelia cardinalis)*. It grows naturally in and around bogs and similar wet spots and requires constant moisture.

 The best solution for wet or poorly drained soil is a raised bed. Raised beds can be as simple as mounds of soil that are 6 to 8 inches above the surrounding soil level, or they can be more complex affairs, utilizing boards, stones, or similar materials to make a soil-retaining border. (See the section "Bailing out with raised beds" later in this chapter.)

Making the Bed

Before you dig in to your gardening project, get all your materials together — soil amendments, fertilizer, digging tools (shovel, digging fork, and a dirt rake or hoe), work gloves, a garden hose, and perhaps a wheelbarrow or garden cart, if you plan to do some really serious digging.

1. **Mark off the area you want to dig, for example by using sticks and twine, as shown in Figure 6-2.**

2. **For your first pass, start at the edge of your bed with a flat-tipped spade and skim an inch or two below the surface, stripping off the sod as shown in Figure 6-3.**

3. **After removing the sod, use a shovel or digging fork to turn the soil, as shown in Figure 6-4.**

   Lift up a spadeful of soil and drop it back onto the ground upside-down. Pull out weeds that come loose and toss them into a pile. When you've turned up the entire bed, take a break — you earned it.

   At this point, if you're unlucky, you may discover that just a few inches below the surface, your soil changes color and becomes very hard. This means that you're working in a site that has only a thin layer of topsoil. That hard stuff is called *hardpan*. See the sidebar, "Double-digging away your hardpan blues," later in this chapter, for advice on handling this situation.

Figure 6-2: Marking off the area you plan to make into a flower bed keeps you from getting carried away with your digging.

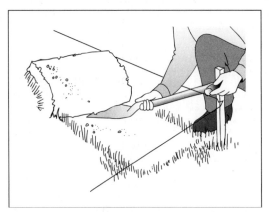

Figure 6-3: Skimming off the sod and setting it aside helps keep grass and weed roots from resprouting and taking over your garden.

Figure 6-4: Breaking up clods of dirt helps to aerate the soil and make a soft base in which young flower roots can grow.

4. **Next, using a hoe or rake, hack away at the big clods to break them up, pulling out weeds as you work.**

5. **Pour on your soil amendments and fertilizer.**

6. **Dig through the bed again with your shovel, working in the amendments and fertilizer.**

   The job of digging the bed is much easier the second time!

7. **Rake over the bed vigorously with a stiff-tined rake to break up clods.**

   Your amended, fertilized, cushion-soft flower bed now needs only a bit of polishing before you start planting. Rake the bed so that it has a level top and slightly sloped sides (as shown in Figure 6-5). If you like, you can make a little lip around the top inside edge to help hold water, at least until the lip washes away.

If you have a dog or cat who has been watching from the sidelines and is poised to continue cultivating your bed as soon as you go inside to rest, sprinkle the surface lightly with cayenne pepper. Martha and Marlon will certainly sniff before they start digging, and one sniff is all it should take to make them change their minds.

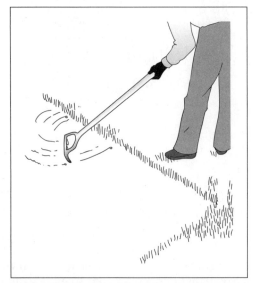

Figure 6-5: Leveling your flower bed not only makes it look pretty, but also helps water to get evenly distributed.

Time for a tiller

Digging a small flower bed is a good exercise program, but preparing a large one by hand can be torture without the help of a tiller. If your bed is larger than 40 square feet (say 10 feet long and 4 feet wide), consider renting, borrowing, or buying a tiller. Rear-tined tillers are generally easier to handle than those with digging tines on the front, but any tiller can really wear you down when you need to jockey it around corners and turns. Tillers work best when they're going in a straight line.

Another option is to have someone else till your flower bed for you. No matter where you live, someone in your community is sure to sell tilling services in the spring. Look in the classified ads in the newspaper or call local garden centers to find this most valuable resource person.

Looking out or looking in: Planting annuals in window boxes adds color to your home, indoors and out. Consider the view from inside when planting near windows.

Ageratum, or floss flower: *Ageratum haustonianum.*

Calendula,
or pot marigold:
Calendula officinalis.

Coleus: *Coleus.*

© David Cavagnaro

© Jerry Pavia

Impatiens: *Impatiens walleriana* 'Super Elfin Twilight.'

Marigold, Signet: *Tagetes tenufolia*.

Morning glory: *Ipomoea imperialis*.

Pansy: *Viola wittrockiana.*

Petunia: *Petunia milliflora.*

Strawflower: *Helichrysum bracteatum.*

© JERRY PAVIA

Sunflower:
Helianthus annus.

© CRANDALL & CRANDALL

Zinnia, mild climate perennial: *Zinnia angustifolia* 'White Star.'

Zinnia, annual: *Zinnia elegans.*

Plant annuals in tiers for levels of color; low in the front, and tall in the back. This garden starts low with petunias and moves up to globe amaranth, salvia,

Double-digging away your hardpan blues

A hard layer of subsoil is a very bad thing if it is within 10 inches of the surface. Besides being so stiff that plant roots cannot penetrate it, subsoil may block the flow of water through the soil and create a drainage problem.

The best remedy for the problem of hard subsoil is called *double-digging*, but you can call it the French Intensive Method if you want to impress people. To do it, put your topsoil in a wheelbarrow or garden cart or pile it up just outside the edge of your bed. With all the energy you can muster, dig up the subsoil, too. If it is tight clay subsoil, you may need a *pick* (the tool that miners use) to break it up. Remove the subsoil to the other side of your bed and keep working until you have a huge hole at least 15 inches deep. Now put your topsoil into the bottom of the bed and layer in huge helpings of soil amendments as you return the subsoil to the topmost layer. By the time you're finished, you will have incorporated so much air and organic matter into the soil that the bed will be raised up several inches higher than the surrounding ground. You also have permanently improved the site and may never need to double-dig it again.

Bailing out with raised beds

Raised beds are a little harder to set up than containers, but they are a fine solution to hardpan and other situations where working the soil is not a viable option.

If you plan to build a raised bed and fill it with bagged soil, plan to make it about 10 inches high. You can enclose your bed with concrete blocks, landscaping timbers, or nifty new boards made from recycled plastic, which fit together via plastic corner brackets. Plastic raised-bed kits come in several shapes and sizes and can be taken apart and moved in a few minutes. Figure 6-6 shows examples of raised-bed options.

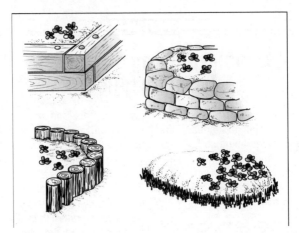

Figure 6-6: Raising your flower bed enables you to use exactly the soil you want, no matter what kind of ground your yard is blessed with.

Whatever material you use to enclose your raised bed, you need enough topsoil (or mixture of soil, compost, humus, and manure) to reach to the top of the frame. Don't worry if the soil heaps up over the edge, because the first time you water, the soil will begin to settle. After a week or so, the soil level will probably be 2 inches below the rim — just the right margin for adding a little mulch when the time comes.

Chapter 7

Planting Seedlings

*T*he quickest way to paint your yard with color is to add some ready-grown annuals to your landscape. Generations of nursery professionals and home gardeners have called these flowers *bedding plants* — a name that suggests their most typical use in the garden. You can find these flowers from spring through summer (or all year 'round in mild climates) at garden centers and nurseries, which pave their sidewalks with bedding plants in three-, four-, and six-packs, or pots of various sizes. And several seed catalogs now sell these flower seedlings by mail.

Some of the flowers commonly offered as bedding plants are simple to start from seed, and it's up to you to decide whether you want to take the time and effort to raise your own seedlings or purchase them. Marigolds, sweet alyssum, and calendula, for example, are easy to grow from seed and reach transplant size in just 6 to 8 weeks. Begonias, impatiens, pansies, and petunias, on the other hand, take up to 12 weeks to grow from seeds to transplanting size.

You can't beat the convenience of purchasing your bedding plants already sprouted. In one afternoon, you can transform a patch of soil into a lush and colorful garden. Visiting local gardening centers and stocking up on flower seedlings is a springtime ritual in many cold-winter regions.

Shopping for Seedlings

The bedding plant industry takes some of the guesswork out of shopping for seedlings by shipping plants to nurseries and garden centers at the best time to plant them. Early in the spring and again in the fall, expect to find annuals that grow best in cool conditions. Annuals that require warmer weather generally arrive later in the spring and keep coming as long as customers keep buying. Remember, however, that nurseries can't predict the weather. You need to be prepared to protect tender seedlings from any late frosts.

The following lists show the availability of some of the most popular bedding plants in the spring. The plants that are available in your area and their estimated arrival time depend on your climate. See Chapter 3 or Chapter 4 for more information about when to plant different annuals in your region.

Popular Bedding Plants Sold in Early Spring	*Popular Bedding Plants Sold in Late Spring*
Calendula	Ageratum
Pink	Begonia
Lobelia	Celosia
Pansy	Dusty miller
Snapdragon	Geranium
Sweet alyssum	Impatiens
Verbena	Marigold
	Petunia
	Salvia
	Vinca rosea

To make sure that you get a healthy plant, check the way the store displays its annuals: Are all the flowers simply lined up in the blazing sun, or have shade-lovers, such as coleus and impatiens, been protected from the sun? Most bedding plants, including those that grow best when they're planted in full sun, do better when kept in partial shade until they're planted.

Be sure to protect your plants as you tote them home in your car. You wouldn't leave the family dog locked up in a hot car with the windows rolled up, so don't treat your plants that way, either.

Nurseries sell annuals in containers of all sizes. Figure 7-1 shows the most common sizes. If you're looking for immediate impact in a flower bed or container, you may want to purchase annuals grown in 4- to 6-inch (or larger) pots. Plants grown in smaller containers take longer to fill their allotted space; however, they cost significantly less than those in larger pots, so if you can be patient, they may be a better choice.

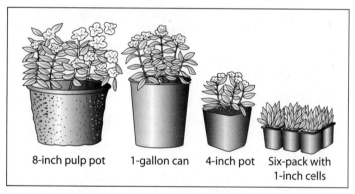

8-inch pulp pot   1-gallon can   4-inch pot   Six-pack with 1-inch cells

Figure 7-1: Choose pot size according to your plans, patience, and budget.

As you shop, look for bedding annuals that are a good green color, appear to have been watered regularly, and are relatively short and stocky. Although it's tempting to pick out the largest plants with the most flowers, these plants may have grown too large for their containers and will suffer during transplanting. You're better off choosing a healthy, compact plant with few or no flowers. These youngsters transplant better and quickly catch up to larger plants.

Avoid large plants growing in small pots. If a plant's roots entirely fill its container and are poking out of the drainage holes, it may be *rootbound,* meaning that the roots have begun to grow in a tight spiral around the perimeter of the pot and may refuse to spread outward after transplanting, stunting the plant's growth.

 At the nursery, don't be shy about tipping the plant out of its pot or pack and inspecting its roots. Avoid plants with thick tangles of root searching for a place to grow — such as out through the container's drainage hole.

Preventing Transplant Shock by Hardening Off

Seedlings that you purchase directly from a greenhouse benefit from a short period of hardening off. (Sounds like the Marine Corps, doesn't it?) *Hardening off* simply means acclimating the seedling to its new surroundings and giving it a chance to adjust to the difference between the comforts of a greenhouse and the cold or heat of an exposed garden bed.

As soon as you get your seedlings home, place them in a bright place that is protected from direct midday sun and strong winds, and water them well. After a few days, move them to full sun. Remember, however, that small pots can dry out very quickly in the midday sun. If you won't be around to check your seedlings every few hours, it's better to leave them in a protected spot until you're ready to transplant. Give them a boost by adding some water-soluble fertilizer next time you give them a drink; choose an all-purpose flower fertilizer and follow label directions. By this time, your seedlings should be nicely accustomed to direct sun and wind and be tough enough to transplant.

If your new seedlings have already spent some time outdoors at the nursery or garden center, they can skip the hardening off and go straight into your garden. Ask the garden center staff whether the seedlings have been hardened off and are ready for transplanting.

TIP

Babes in bloom

Statistics show that consumers are much more likely to buy plants that are already in flower. As a result, plant breeders have tinkered with genes to develop flowers that pop a blossom or two at an early age and then devote a few more weeks to vegetative growth before they start blooming again.

If you buy plants already in flower, pinch off the blossom when you set out the plants — unless you're having guests for dinner, in which case you can wait until the next day. This preemptive pinching encourages the plants to get on with the business of growing buds and branches.

Planning to Plant: Give 'em Some Elbow Room

Gardeners tend to have very tight plant spacing in window boxes and containers, but in open beds, the best strategy is to space seedlings so that they will barely touch each other when they reach full maturity. Because different annual flowers grow to different sizes, the amount of space they require varies.

Very small annuals, such as sweet alyssum and lobelia, can be spaced only 4 to 6 inches apart, but big coleus and celosia may do better if they're placed 18 inches apart. Most other annuals grow best planted about 10 to 12 inches apart. The plant tags tucked into the containers of bedding plants often suggest the best spacing.

Instead of setting your annuals in straight lines, try staggering them in a concentrated zigzag pattern so that you have two or more offset rows of plants. This planting design fills a large space more uniformly and looks less rigid than plants lined up in rows. Better yet, plant groups of similar annuals in teardrop-shaped clumps (called *drifts*); this design often looks more natural and helps create focal points in the design. The clump approach also makes many flowers easier to care for. Pinching, pruning, and giving extra water and fertilizer to a closely spaced group of plants is easier than ministering to a long row of flowers.

When planning your planting arrangement, you can estimate the plant spacing and simply make little holes in the prepared bed where you intend to set the plants. Or you can mark the planting spots with craft sticks or lightly dust each spot with plain all-purpose flour. If you already purchased plants in individual containers, simply place the plants where you intend to plant them, and move them around as needed until you're happy with the arrangement.

Planting Seedlings, Step by Step

Whether you buy your seedlings or grow them from seeds, follow these steps to ensure that your plants get off to a good start in your garden.

 Transplant during cloudy weather or late in the day. Hot sun during transplanting causes unnecessary stress to the little plants.

1. **The day before transplanting, water the planting bed so that it will be lightly moist when you set out your plants.**

2. **Water your seedlings thoroughly a few hours before transplanting.**

Extras and understudies

Frequently, after planting your garden, you end up with a few extra bedding plants. Don't throw them away. If your garden follows a formal design, where even one additional plant would stand out, transplant the extras to slightly larger individual pots. This way, if a few plants spontaneously expire or get dug up by your neighbor's dog, you can quickly plug in a replacement that's an exact match.

Another way to use annual orphans is to plant them together in large containers. Place the tallest, most upright flowers in the middle and surround them with smaller plants. In a few weeks, you'll have a remarkably pretty container bouquet that looks like you spent hours designing it.

Watering the seedlings makes them much easier to remove from their containers.

3. **Carefully remove the seedling from the container.**

   If small roots are knotted around the outside of the drainage holes, pinch off the roots and discard them before trying to remove the plants. Then push and squeeze on the bottom of the container to make the entire root ball slip out intact, as shown in Figure 7-2. If it won't come out easily, use a table knife to gently pry it out, the same way you might remove a sticky cake from a pan. Pull on the top of the plant only as a last resort.

Figure 7-2: Push seedlings out of their container by pressing lightly on the bottom of their pot. Avoid pulling on them from above.

4. **Gently tease apart roots.**

   Use your fingers or a table fork to loosen the tangle of roots at the bottom of the root ball, as shown in Figure 7-3. This step encourages the roots to spread out into the surrounding soil.

Figure 7-3: Breaking a few roots won't hurt the plant, as long as the mass of roots remains intact.

5. **Make final spacing decisions and dig planting holes slightly larger than the root balls of the plants.**

   Set the plants in the holes at the same depth they grew in their containers, as shown in Figure 7-4.

6. **Lightly firm soil around the roots with your hands, as shown in Figure 7-5.**

   Removing air pockets helps secure the plant's roots.

7. **If you want, mix a batch of balanced or high-phosphorus, water- soluble fertilizer and give each plant a good slurp.**

   High-phosphorus fertilizers have a large middle number, such as 5-7-4. If you mixed in fertilizer while preparing the planting bed, you shouldn't have to feed your plants again now. (For more about fertilizing annuals, see Chapter 9.)

8. **Gently water the entire bed until it's evenly moist but not muddy, as shown in Figure 7-6.**

   Because you watered the bed before planting (Step 1), the intent is to help the soil settle around the plants' roots. Use a hose with a bubbler nozzle, a sprinkler, or a watering can rosette-type spout. Take care not to wash away surface soil, leaving roots exposed.

Figure 7-4: Scoop a trowelful of soil to one side so that the hole is just deep enough to accommodate the seedling.

Figure 7-5: Firm soil around a young plant just enough so that it can remain upright.

Figure 7-6: Use a gentle shower of water, rather than a strong jet-stream, on newly planted annuals.

9. **After a few days, check to make sure that soil has not washed away from the top of the plants' roots.**

   If it has, use a rake or small trowel to level the soil around the plants.

10. **As soon as new growth shows, mulch around plants with an attractive mulch, such as shredded bark, pine needles, or shredded leaves.**

    A 2- to 3-inch layer of mulch discourages weeds and radically reduces moisture loss from the soil due to evaporation. Turn to Chapter 11 to find out about the different types of mulch and how to use them.

Special care for beautiful beds

Given warm sun and ample water, most annuals speed right along and come into full bloom in a few short weeks. If you live in a dry area where watering is likely to eat up all your spare time, give some thought to rigging up an irrigation system for your annual flower bed. A series of inexpensive soaker hoses hidden under the mulch can make watering a simple matter of turning on the faucet at very low pressure for a few hours a couple of times each week. For more details on watering, check out Chapter 8.

Dwarf varieties of most annual flowers need no pinching right after transplanting, for their natural tendency is to develop numerous branches that emerge from the main stem near the soil line. However, flowers that tend to grow upright, such as snapdragons, tall zinnias, and marigolds, grow bushier if you clip or pinch off the topmost growing tip a week or so after transplanting. If necessary, use scissors or pruning shears so that you don't have to twist and pull to remove the growing tip. If it breaks your heart to pinch off the tip, wait until the first flower opens and promptly cut it and put it in a vase. New branches and buds should quickly pop out from the largest stems of the sheared plant.

Year-round beds

In climates with very long growing seasons, annual beds are often "turned over" two or three times a year. For example, if you live in a warm region where winters don't freeze at all, or where they freeze only slightly (such as southern Texas or Palm Springs, California), you can plant pansies in the fall and enjoy them until May. By then, the pansies are pooped, and it's time to replace them with something new. With a little planning, you can complete such a garden renovation very quickly by following these steps:

1. **Dampen the soil to make the old plants easy to pull out.**

2. **Grab the plants close to the soil and pull to get as many of the roots as you can.**

   Throw out the roots or toss them into a compost heap, if you have one.

3. **Spread a 2-inch layer of compost or composted manure and a light dusting of a balanced time-release or organic fertilizer over the empty section of your bed.**

4. **Dig or till the bed as needed to mix in the compost and fertilizer, and rake the soil smooth.**

   You're now ready to install a new crop of annuals. Simply follow the steps under "Planting Seedlings, Step by Step."

Chapter 8

Quenching Your Flowers' Thirst

- -

In This Chapter

▶ Looking at the factors that affect an annual's water needs

▶ Comparing different watering methods

▶ Knowing how often to water

▶ Deciding how much to water

▶ Conserving water

- -

*L*ike many plants, annuals need consistent moisture in the soil in order to grow and bloom beautifully. But the trick is knowing how to get that moisture in the soil and how much of it to apply. In fact, watering may be one of the trickiest aspects of growing annual flowers.

Unlike many plants, annuals are not very forgiving if they don't get the water they want, when they want it. If you let some of these finicky plants dry out, they'll stop growing and quit blooming for good. (Drowning your plants has that same effect.) If they don't die, most under- or overwatered annuals at least shut down for a while. For a more permanent plant, a temporary halt in growth may not be the end of the world. But with annuals, fast, consistent growth is critical. If the plant stalls, you may lose a good part, if not all, of the blooming season.

This chapter shows you how to water wisely and keep your annuals growing strong all season long. No matter what watering method or tools you employ, the most important rule of watering is to observe your plants and soil on a regular basis and respond appropriately to what they're telling you.

Determining a Plant's Water Needs

The amount of water that annuals need to stay healthy and full of blooms depends on a number of factors, including climate, weather, soil type, garden location, and type of annuals used.

Considering climate

The climate of an area encompasses a wide range of factors, such as the amount of average rainfall, the high and low temperatures, the relative humidity, and the amount of wind. If you live in an area where rainfall is regular and reliable (like Seattle, Washington; Vancouver, British Columbia; London, England; or Biloxi, Mississippi) watering isn't a constant chore, except during prolonged dry spells or periods of drought. In drier areas, such as Los Angeles, California, and Phoenix, Arizona, watering is a task you must squeeze into your schedule almost on a daily basis.

You have to water container-grown annuals even more frequently than your plants in the ground. In fact, daily watering of annuals in containers is essential in almost all climates during certain times of the year.

Watching the weather

Climate is determined by the average weather where you live on a season-to-season, year-to-year basis. Weather is what's happening outside at any given moment. Out-of-the-ordinary weather can wreak havoc on your plants. Hot, dry winds can fry annuals even when the soil is moist. Prolonged rain can turn zinnias to mush, rot the roots of vinca rosea, and turn cosmos into a mildewy mess.

Table 8-1 shows, in a nutshell, guidelines on how to adjust watering according to weather conditions.

Table 8-1	Watering According to Weather
Water Less	*Water More*
Cooler temperatures	Warmer temperatures
Cloudy or overcast	Bright sunshine
Low wind	High wind
High humidity	Low humidity
Rain	No rain

Studying your soil

Different soil types affect how often a garden needs water. For example, sand holds water about as effectively as a sieve. Water penetrates sandy soil readily and deeply, but tends to filter right on through. Therefore, you need to water plants in sandy soil more frequently than plants in clay soil.

Heavy clay is the exact opposite. Its dense particles crust over and deflect water drops. If you apply water slowly and in stages, it soaks in; if you apply it quickly and all at once, it just runs off. But after clay is saturated, it holds water very well — sometimes so well that the plants rot.

Luckily, when you grow annuals, you can amend the soil with organic matter on a yearly, if not seasonal, basis. Adding organic matter, such as compost, leaf mold, or ground bark, helps sandy soils to retain moisture and helps break up clay soils to improve aeration and drainage. (See Chapter 6 for more information on improving sandy or clay soils.)

Looking at location

In general, shady gardens need less water than those planted in direct sunlight. By blocking the sun's heat, shade cuts down on the amount of water that evaporates from the soil.

However, in places where trees are responsible for casting the shadow, the tree roots may be greedily hogging all the water, leaving little for the flowers. Maples in particular have roots so close to the surface that it's almost impossible to apply enough water to satisfy the tree and the flowers. The farther from the trunk of the tree you place your flowers, the more room they have to spread their roots, and the less they have to compete with the tree for water and nutrients.

If you plan to plant in a shady area, choose annuals that don't need direct sunlight to thrive. Impatiens, forget-me-nots, and browallia are good choices for the dark corners of your yard.

Picking your plants

Although most annual flowers need a consistent supply of moisture to remain healthy and free-blooming, some annuals can get by on less water than others. For example, California poppies, gazanias, portulaca, salvia, and verbena adapt fairly well to hot, dry conditions. Vinca rosea and snapdragons are very sensitive to overly wet soils and can rot if their roots are not allowed to partially dry out between waterings.

Still other annuals, such as impatiens, can survive through occasional dry spells, but they look terrible and stop blooming until they receive the water they need.

Read up on the water requirements of the plants you like and then decide whether you can modify your soil or site to accommodate them. Aside from amending your soil, you can group plants according to their water needs. For example, plant a flower that wilts rapidly when it's deprived of water in a location that's partially shaded by other plants during the blazing heat of late afternoon. If you garden in containers, you have much more control because you can move the pots around if your plants begin to complain about their present location.

Checking Out the Ways to Water

You can choose from a number of ways to apply water to your flowers. Some methods are better than others, but often the best method depends on the size of your flower garden. For example, if you have a small bed of marigolds, a handheld watering can may be all you need. If, however, you have a 200-square-foot flower bed, watering effectively by hand is not just impractical, it's impossible.

Knowing when to water

The water needs of your annuals vary with the weather and the seasons. You must learn to be a pretty good observer and make adjustments accordingly.

However, here are some easy ways to tell when your plants need water:

✔ Look at your plants. Your annual has ways of telling you when it's thirsty. When an annual starts to dry out, the leaves get droopy and wilt. The plant may also lose its bright green color and start to look a little drab. Your goal is to water before a plant reaches that

point, but the plant will tell you when it needs water more often.

✔ Dig in the ground. Most annuals need water when the top two to three inches of soil are dry. So take a small trowel or shovel and dig around a bit. If the top of the soil is dry, it's time to water.

Eventually, through observation and digging, you start to develop a watering schedule, and you can eliminate some of the guesswork from this part of your gardening routine.

In some areas, certain watering techniques become a matter of necessity instead of practicality. In regions where droughts are common or water supplies are unpredictable, conservation is the order of the day. You need to water in ways that hold every drop precious. If foliage diseases such as powdery mildew are common, keep water off the plant leaves and apply it only to the roots. (See Chapter 12 for more information on powdery mildew and other plant diseases.)

Hand watering

If you want to stand around with a hose and water by hand, that's fine. In fact, container gardens require hand watering (that is, unless you install a sophisticated drip-irrigation system). You can buy small hose-end attachments to control the flow of water that gurgles out of your hose. Small hose-end bubblers soften the spray of water; spray wands (Figure 8-1) increase the water pressure for larger areas.

Figure 8-1: A spray wand on an extension tube lets you reach hanging baskets without washing away the soil.

But hand watering takes time, especially in large gardens, and the time and boredom factors often tempt you to stop watering before your plants have received enough water. Most plants prefer a good soaking every couple of days to a light sprinkling every day. Be sure to water long enough that moisture reaches down to the root zone of the plants.

Sprinklers

Many types of hose-end sprinklers are available, and you've probably used a few of them in your day (even if it was just to play in the arcs of water). The problem with using sprinklers to water your flower beds is that you have to drag the hose all around and frequently move the sprinkler. In addition, most hose-end sprinklers don't apply water very evenly. And if you forget to turn off the sprinkler, you waste a lot of water (though you can solve this problem by installing an automatic timer between the faucet and the hose).

Choose a sprinkler that emits the largest droplets possible because, on a hot day, tiny drops can evaporate before they even reach the ground. Look for a sprinkler that covers a wide area and avoid those that send water straight up into the air (where it can evaporate more quickly).

Sprinklers work best when every flower is the same height. Otherwise, the taller plants get in the way of the spray pattern. In fact, overhead watering can weigh down some taller annuals, such as cosmos, and cause them to flop over on the ground.

You may encounter another possible problem from overhead watering and the resulting wet foliage. In humid climates, overhead watering can spread disease and turn your flowers into a moldy mess. On the other hand, in hot, dry climates, wetting the foliage rinses dust off the leaves and helps prevent spider mite infestations.

The automated system

Automated watering systems can be real time-savers and can give you the freedom to safely take a vacation in the middle of summer. By operating on a timer hooked up to your faucet, these systems turn on and off by themselves at preset intervals. You can find an interesting mixture of timers at your local irrigation supplier or in mail-order catalogs.

Some timers are hooked between the end of the faucet and the hose, and others are connected to valves and underground pipes that supply sprinklers. You can even build a moisture sensor into an automated system so that the water comes on only when the soil is dry. (Isn't technology wonderful?) Both drip and sprinkler systems can be fully automated.

Just remember, even an automated system needs to be adjusted to water less in the spring than in the summer.

If you do use sprinklers, don't put them in the same place every time you water. And even during a single watering, move the sprinklers around so that your flowers are evenly watered.

Furrow irrigation

Furrows are shallow trenches that run parallel to your rows of flowers. (See Figure 8-2.) Usually you dig them with a hoe at planting time and then plant a row of flowers on either side of the furrow. Ideally, the flower bed should be sloped just the tiniest bit so that water runs naturally from one end of the furrow to the other. When you want to water, you simply put a slowly running hose at the end of the furrow and wait for the water to reach the other end.

Figure 8-2: Furrow irrigation makes use of gravity to carry water from one end of the furrow to the other.

Furrow irrigation keeps the foliage dry, and therefore doesn't promote disease the way sprinkler watering does. However, you do have to drag the hose from furrow to furrow. And this type of system doesn't work well on fast-draining, sandy soil. The water soaks in too quickly and never reaches the other end.

Drip irrigation

Drip irrigation is a very effective and efficient way to water annuals. It works well even if your garden is on a slope, which poses a problem for some other systems. Drip irrigation provides water slowly through holes or emitters in a flexible black plastic pipe. You weave this pipe (which is connected to a water supply, a filter, and often a pressure regulator) along the rows of plants so that the water flows directly to the bases of the flowers, as shown in Figure 8-3.

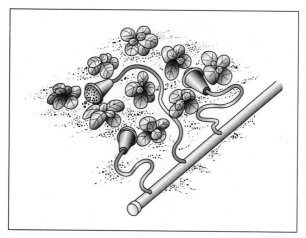

Figure 8-3: Drip irrigation slowly delivers water precisely where you need it, so less is lost to evaporation and runoff.

You can wet an entire bed from one end to the other at each watering with drip emitters. (You can snap the emitters in the pipe wherever you want them, or you can buy pipe with the emitters already evenly spaced along the length of the pipe.) The moisture radiates sideways underground and wets the soil between emitters.

You can lay the pipe right on top of the soil and cover it with a mulch, or you can bury the pipe a few inches below the surface of the soil. Most people like to keep the pipe close to the surface so that they can check it for clogs and fix breaks.

You usually have to run drip systems for at least several hours to wet a large area. Watch the system carefully the first few times you water. Dig around to see how far the water has traveled over a given time. Then make adjustments in your watering schedule in the future.

If you live in an area where the soil freezes, don't leave your drip system outside in winter. It may burst. Instead, drain the water out, roll up the tubing, and store it in the garage.

Most nurseries sell drip irrigation systems. You can also purchase them through the mail. Emitters are available with different application rates, varying by the number of gallons applied per hour. Pressure-compensating emitters apply water consistently from one end of the line to the other, regardless of pressure changes due to uneven ground.

Soaker-hose irrigation

A soaker-hose system consists of a rubber hose perforated with tiny pores that leak water. You can lay the hose in rows or curve it around plants, similar to the drip irrigation system. Water leaks out of the hose and into the soil, leaving the plant leaves dry and reducing evaporation. A soaker-hose system is simpler than drip irrigation because it involves fewer parts and no nozzles. Its primary limitation is that it works best on flat terrain, often delivering water unevenly in a sloped garden.

Keep your garden looking tidy and improve the efficiency of your soaker hose by laying it on top of the soil and covering it with mulch. You can easily customize a system to fit your garden by threading the hose around your plantings, as shown in Figure 8-4.

Figure 8-4: Soaker hoses are flexible enough to curve around your plants.

How Much Water to Apply

The roots of most annuals grow in the top 8 to 10 inches of soil. That's where the soil is well aerated and conditions suit root growth. When you water, therefore, you must make sure that the moisture reaches a depth of 8 to 10 inches. If you water any shallower, the roots won't be able to grow deeply because they just won't penetrate the dry soil. Shallow-rooted plants are more susceptible to fluctuations in soil moisture because they don't have a large soil reserve to draw from. Bottom line: Don't sprinkle lightly. It does little good.

On the other hand, you don't need to apply so much water that it goes deeper than 8 to 10 inches. Not many roots are growing at that depth, so you'd only be wasting water.

So how do you tell how deep you're watering? Get out your trusty trowel or shovel and dig in an open area of your flower bed. If the water hasn't reached deep enough, water longer. If the soil is still soaking wet at a foot deep, you can cut back some.

Water-saving tips

Water shortages are a reality in almost any climate or region. Here are a few things you can do when water is scarce or limited, when you want to reduce your water bill, or when you just want to conserve the precious resource of fresh water.

✔ **Use a timer.** If you've ever forgotten to turn the water off and ended up flooding half the neighborhood, this tip's for you. Just set an egg timer or an alarm clock to let you know when to shut off the water. Or you can get even more high-tech and use one of the automated timers that I describe in the section "Checking Out the Ways to Water."

✔ **Install drip irrigation.** This method applies water slowly without runoff. Drip is definitely the most frugal watering system you can use.

✔ **Mulch, mulch, and mulch some more.** A mulch is a layer of organic matter that you spread over the root zone beneath a plant. Several inches of compost, shredded fir bark, leaf mold, or other material cool the soil and reduce evaporation, thus saving water. And as the mulch breaks down, it improves the soil. For more on mulches, see Chapter 11.

✔ **Pull weeds.** Weeds steal water meant for your annuals, so keep them pulled. For more on weeds, see Chapter 11.

✔ **Water deeply and infrequently.** Shallow sprinkling does very little good. Water to a depth of 8 to 10 inches and then let the soil dry out partially before you water again. This way, you develop deep roots that can go longer between waterings.

✔ **Use rainwater.** Put a barrel or other collector where the drain pipes from your roof empty. Then use that water on your flowers.

✔ **Measure rainfall.** Keep track of how much rain you get with a rain gauge, available from garden centers and hardware stores. An inch of rain at one time is usually enough to let you skip a watering.

✔ **Plant at the right time.** Plant when your annuals have the best chance of getting fully established before the onset of hot weather. For proper planting times for your area, see Chapters 3 and 4.

✔ **Plant drought-tolerant annuals.** I mention a few camels of the annual world earlier in this chapter, in the section "Determining a Plant's Water Needs."

Chapter 9

Feeding Those Hungry Annuals

In This Chapter

▶ Supplying nutrients for healthy growth

▶ Reading a fertilizer label

▶ Shopping for fertilizers

▶ Knowing how much and how often to fertilize annuals

▶ Fertilizing annuals in containers

▶ Using organic fertilizers

*I*f annuals are flowering powerhouses (and they are), then fertilizer is the coal that fuels the powerhouse. If you don't create enough steam, the power won't be there and blooming will be sparse. If you create too much steam, the whole thing blows up and you fry the plants.

Proper fertilization, especially when annuals are young, is very important to the quality of bloom. Even though young transplants or seedlings may not be blooming much, their growth during the first six to eight weeks after planting has a huge impact on how well they bloom later. Keeping annuals growing vigorously, never letting them stall, and building healthy foliage early on results in spectacular power when they're ready to bloom. And after annuals have started blooming, proper fertilization keeps them blooming as long as possible.

This chapter covers the what, the how much, and the how often of fertilizing annuals. Get ready to stoke those fires.

In Need of Nutrients

Plants need 16 different elements for healthy growth. Carbon, hydrogen, and oxygen — the foundation blocks for photosynthesis — are required in large quantities, but nature or your watering hose automatically provides these elements.

Plants also need relatively large amounts of nitrogen, phosphorus, and potassium, which are called *macronutrients*. Plants require *secondary nutrients* (calcium, magnesium, and sulfur) in smaller quantities and need the *micronutrients* (iron, manganese, copper, boron, molybdenum, chlorine, and zinc) in even smaller amounts.

Macronutrients, secondary nutrients, and micronutrients are mostly absorbed from the soil by plant roots. If any nutrient is not present in the soil in sufficient quantities, or is present in a form that the plant can't absorb, you must add it as fertilizer or correct the conditions that make it difficult for the nutrient to be absorbed.

Luckily, most soils already contain enough nutrients for healthy growth. In fact, when growing annual flowers, many gardeners may find that nitrogen is the only element that they need to apply via fertilizers. But how do you know for sure? You can look for yellowing of the lower leaves (a sure sign of nitrogen deficiency), but to be absolutely sure that the problem is lack of nitrogen, you can have your soil tested. A soil test, discussed in detail in Chapter 6, reveals which nutrients are or aren't present in your soil so that you can know the type and quantity of fertilizer to apply.

But a soil test doesn't provide *all* the answers; it only tells you what to work into your soil *before* planting. You still have to apply nitrogen, and maybe other nutrients, later on. To understand why, you need to know a little more about plant nutrients and how they react with the soil.

Nitrogen — once is not enough

Nitrogen is often the only nutrient that you need to apply as a fertilizer. The reason soil tends to be deficient in nitrogen is that plants use more nitrogen than any other nutrient, so the nitrogen supply is quickly depleted from the soil. Nitrogen is also less stationary in the soil. In other words, it can be washed or leached out of the soil when you water. Phosphorus and potassium are less mobile — so once they're there, they stay put for quite a while.

Why do plants need so much nitrogen? Nitrogen promotes healthy growth. As a key part of plant proteins and *chlorophyll,* the plant pigment that plays a vital role in photosynthesis, nitrogen is responsible for the green color of plant leaves. Plants that are deficient in nitrogen show a yellowing of older leaves first, along with a general slowdown in growth.

If your annuals aren't producing their quota of blooms, the reason is probably that the soil doesn't contain enough nitrogen. Luckily, plants usually respond quickly to nitrogen application, so nitrogen deficiency is easy to correct. How? You guessed it — by adding fertilizer.

Balancing other nutrients

In addition to nitrogen, phosphorus and potassium (the other two macronutrients) also play important roles in plant growth. Phosphorus is associated with good root growth and with flower, fruit, and seed production. Potassium is necessary for healthy roots, disease resistance, and fruiting. Deficiencies in either nutrient are not as obvious as nitrogen deficiency and are therefore harder to detect simply from looking at symptoms on a plant. Only a soil test can tell for sure.

Because phosphorus and potassium are less mobile than nitrogen, you can't just water them in to the soil as you can with nitrogen. Instead, you have to work those nutrients into the soil at planting time. That way, they're located right where the roots can absorb them.

Determining the secondary nutrients and the micronutrients that your plants need is also hard, if not impossible, without a soil test. Some of the nutrients may be present, but the *pH,* or the relative acidity or alkalinity, of the soil prevents the plants from being able to absorb them. In such a case, that good old soil test tells you how to adjust your soil pH so that the nutrients can be absorbed. You can find out more about soil pH in Chapter 6.

Shopping for Fertilizers

At first glance, a nursery shelf full of fertilizers is an overwhelming sight. But it really doesn't have to be so confusing. Among all the colorful bags, bottles, and jars, you can find a consistency in labeling to guide you through much of the confusion and lead you to the fertilizer that's best for your annuals.

Checking the guaranteed analysis

When you buy a commercial fertilizer, look on the label for three numbers separated by dashes, as shown in Figure 9-1. These three numbers are a fertilizer's *guaranteed analysis,* telling you how much of each of the macronutrients the fertilizer contains.

- The first number indicates the percentage of nitrogen (N).
- The second number indicates the percentage of phosphate (P_2O_5).
- The third number indicates the percentage of potash (K_2O), which is another name for potassium.

For example, a 10-8-6 fertilizer is 10 percent nitrogen, 8 percent phosphorus (a form of phosphate), and 6 percent potash.

Do the math, and you see that a 100-pound bag of 10-5-5 fertilizer contains 10 pounds of nitrogen, 5 pounds of phosphorus, and 5 pounds of potash — a total of 20 pounds of usable nutrients. Although the remaining 80 pounds contains a small amount of other useful nutrients (also listed on the label), most of the extra bulk is just filler left over from manufacturing.

Figure 9-1: All fertilizer labels show the percentage of nitrogen, phosphorus, and potash (potassium).

Considering other factors

The guaranteed analysis is your primary shopping guide when buying fertilizer. But you may want to recognize some of the different types of fertilizers and understand more fertilizer-related terminology before you begin filling your cart:

✔ **Granular fertilizers:** The most common type of fertilizer, granular fertilizers come in bags or boxes and are either partially or completely soluble. They can be scattered over the soil and watered in, or worked into the soil before planting. You can mix the completely soluble types with water and apply them when you irrigate.

✔ **Liquid fertilizers:** You can buy this type of fertilizer in bottles or jugs. On a per-nutrient basis, most liquid fertilizers are more expensive than granular ones. Most liquid fertilizers need to be diluted in water before using, but some are ready to use. You apply liquid fertilizers when you water, and you can inject them into irrigation systems, which is the reason that many professional growers prefer them. They are particularly easy to use on plants grown in containers. Some liquid fertilizers are sold in hose-end applicators (shown in Figure 9-2), which eliminate mixing.

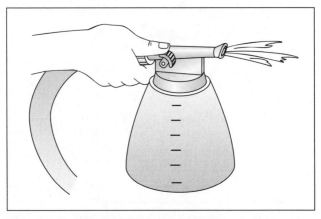

Figure 9-2: Applying liquid fertilizer with a hose-end attachment.

✔ **Chelated micronutrients:** This term refers to nutrients in a form that plants can absorb more quickly than the more commonly available sulfated forms. If, no matter how much nitrogen you apply, your plants just won't green up (they stay mottled yellow and green, or just plain yellow), you probably have a micronutrient deficiency of iron, zinc, or manganese. Chelated micronutrients are the quickest fix, although you may also have a soil pH problem that's preventing the nutrients from being absorbed by the plant. (See Chapter 6 for more information about soil pH.)

✔ **Foliar fertilizers:** This term refers to fertilizers that you apply to the leaves of plants instead of to the roots. That's right, leaves can absorb nutrients, too. Leaves don't absorb nutrients as effectively as roots do, but they do absorb the nutrients quickly — so foliar feeding is a good fast-food fix for your plants. You can use most liquid fertilizers as foliar fertilizers, but make sure that the label indicates that it's okay to do so. Don't apply foliar fertilizers in hot weather, because they may burn the leaves.

✔ **Organic fertilizers:** Fertilizers labeled as *organic* derive their nutrients directly from plant, animal, or mineral sources and tend to have a minimum of refining done during their manufacturing process. Some examples include kelp meal, bonemeal, and greensand. Organic fertilizers tend to have lower amounts of all nutrients, and they often have only one main nutrient; greensand, for example, contains mostly potassium.

To be effective, organic fertilizers need soil containing lots of soil microbes that can break down these products into forms the plant can use. Unlike chemical fertilizers, organic fertilizers make nutrients available to the plant roots slowly over a long period of time — only after the microbes have digested them. Microbes thrive in warm soils with lots of organic matter, such as leaves, grass clippings, and manure. Table 9-1 lists the nutrient contents of the most common organic fertilizers.

✔ **Slow-release fertilizers:** These chemical fertilizers release nutrients slowly in response to specific environmental conditions, such as temperatures or moisture. Slow-release fertilizers come in the form of pellets that are covered with a thin membrane, which slowly breaks down under the right temperature, moisture, or activity from soil microbes. As the membrane dissolves, the fertilizer inside the pellets is gradually released into the soil, for a period of up to eight months. This type of pellet is especially beneficial for the release of nitrogen, which tends to leach easily from the soil. Slow-release (or *time-release,* as they are sometimes called) fertilizers are best used for annuals grown in pots, but they may also be used as a supplement to other fertilizers if you have vigorous free-growing annuals such as morning glories.

Be warned: Slow-release fertilizers are very expensive. And when annuals are growing quickly, they may need more nitrogen than the slow-release fertilizer is providing. Watch your annuals carefully. If they grow slowly or are a bit yellowish in spite of their diet of slow-release fertilizer, give them a boost with an application of regular fertilizer.

✔ **Specialty fertilizers:** This term refers to fertilizers that are supposedly formulated for specific types of plants. For example, you may find a fertilizer labeled Flower Food with an analysis of 0-10-10. The logic behind such a fertilizer is that a blooming plant needs more phosphorus and potassium than it does nitrogen. That's because the phosphorus and potassium are important in the formation of flowers, and the nitrogen promotes the growth of leaves. And you want flowers, right? Well, not so fast. Because phosphorus and potassium don't move into the soil as well as nitrogen does, you can apply all you want of a fertilizer with phosphorus and potassium, and it may not get to the roots. Besides, if your soil test indicated that you have sufficient phosphorus and potassium, adding more does not give you more flowers.

Truth be told, I think specialty fertilizers are more of a marketing strategy than a high-tech solution. They're quite expensive compared to other fertilizers. If your annuals need nitrogen — and they probably do — then nitrogen, and only nitrogen, is what you should apply.

With so many options, how do you know which fertilizer to use on your flower bed? Because annuals aren't particularly fussy, you can use *any* kind of fertilizer that shows a nice balance of the major plant nutrients.

Inexpensive granular fertilizers usually contain only the big guns: nitrogen, phosphorus, and potassium. But why not go high-end with your fertilizer? For a bit more money, you can buy fertilizer that also contains a buffet of micronutrients (such as calcium and magnesium) and is coated to ensure that the nutrients are released very slowly each time you water. If you incorporate one of these slow-release fertilizers into your soil before you plant your flowers, you may never have to think about fertilizer again for the rest of the season.

Fertilizers that are slow-release say so right on the bag. The label also specifies *how* slow the release is. For example, a bag might say "three-month formula," or "six-month formula." Choose the time span that best fits your climate. Where the growing season is only three or four months long, the former is obviously sufficient.

You can use the same approach with balanced organic fertilizers, which are usually bulkier but every bit as good as their chemical counterparts. (In fact, many flower fans who aren't especially concerned about organic practices in their general thinking opt for organic fertilizers for their annual flowers.) Organic fertilizers can be relatively simple concoctions, such as dried, pelleted turkey or chicken manure, or they can be elaborate mixtures of fish meal, bonemeal, feather meal, and even shrimp hulls. You need not worry about possible odors, because you mix the materials into the soil where the smells are hidden from your nose. Because organic fertilizers vary so much in their content and potency, carefully read the label to find out how much you need to use.

Fertilizing Your Flower Bed

The best time to start fertilizing your flower bed is before you start planting. Giving your annuals a nutrient-rich home from the get-go ensures healthy development during their most formative period.

For the best results, add your fertilizer no more than a day or so before planting. Organic matter, such as compost, can be added at any time. Here's a fertilizer plan that works well for me:

1. **Before planting, spread a complete, high-nitrogen, granular fertilizer evenly over the planting area at the rate recommended on the package (usually 2 to 3 cups of fertilizer per 100 square feet).**

   You can do the spreading by hand, but be sure to wear gloves. If a test indicated that your soil has enough phosphorus and potassium, then use a product containing only nitrogen.

   If you're really ambitious and are planting a large bed of annuals, using a broadcaster to spread the fertilizer will make the job much easier. Broadcasters, like the one shown in Figure 9-3, are commonly used for lawn care but are just as effective in large flower beds. Follow the instructions and rates recommended on the packaging (usually 10 to 20 pounds per 1,000 square feet of garden).

Figure 9-3: Using a broadcaster to spread granular fertilizer

2. **Add lime or sulfur to balance your soil's pH.**

   If you discover that your pH needs correcting, apply lime to bring the pH to a more alkaline (higher pH) state, or sulfur to make the pH more acidic (lower). Lime and sulfur are available at garden centers and can be applied either by hand or with a broadcaster like the one shown in Figure 9-3.

3. **Spread a 2- or 3-inch layer of organic matter.**

   The best type of organic matter to spread just before planting is finished compost or composted manure. These are available in bags from garden centers, or you can create your own compost by allowing your organic matter (leaves, manure, grass clippings, and so on) to decompose. See Chapter 6 of this book for the basics of composting or, for detailed instructions, pick up a copy of *Gardening For Dummies* by Michael MacCaskey and the Editors of the National Gardening Association (Wiley).

4. **Work everything into the soil, turning it with a shovel or rotary tiller so that all the nutrients end up where the roots can get them.**

When planting, don't allow the roots of transplants to come in direct contact with the fertilizer. The high nitrogen content may burn the exposed roots.

5. Plant your flower bed.

After planting, be sure to water the bed thoroughly.

6. Every four to six weeks, fertilize again with a high-nitrogen fertilizer.

If you have really sandy soil in which nutrients wash through quickly, you may have to fertilize more often. If plants are slow to respond to these nutrients (say, if you don't see an improvement after a week), apply a foliar fertilizer for an extra boost.

You can use either a liquid or granular fertilizer, but if you use a granular fertilizer, water well after each application, making sure that you wash off any fertilizer that may have settled on the leaves.

Don't fertilize dry plants, or you may do more harm than good. Plants need water to move fertilizer nutrients to the roots and help them take these fertilizers up into the plant. Without adequate water, the plant roots that do contact the fertilizers may be burned, causing the roots to die and the plant to suffer. Always water your plants well before and after fertilizing to get the most benefit from the fertilizer.

Some gardeners prefer to start cutting back on nitrogen after their annuals reach full bloom, thinking that the nitrogen may force leaf growth at the expense of flowers. I don't believe this theory. If you're tending annual flowers properly, by removing spent blooms, for example, consistent applications of nitrogen throughout the life of the plant result in more blooms.

Overfertilizing can be much worse than not applying enough fertilizer. Excess nitrogen, for example, can burn the edges of leaves and even kill a plant. Besides that, if you apply too much fertilizer, it can leach into ground water, and then you're a nasty polluter. So always follow instructions on the fertilizer label and apply only nutrients that you're sure are deficient in your soil — too much of any nutrient can cause problems with plants and the environment. If you have doubts about what your soil needs, have your soil professionally tested.

Fertilizing Annuals in Containers

Plants growing in containers need more water than those growing in the ground. The more you water, the more you flush nutrients from the soil, and the more often you have to fertilize.

 You can offset some of this constant loss of nutrients by mixing slow-release fertilizers into the soil before planting. But I also like to take a less-fertilizer-more-often approach. The best pots of annuals I've seen are on a constant feeding program. In other words, you give your flowers a little liquid fertilizer every time, or every other time, you water them. Cut the recommended rates on the bottle of fertilizer in half or into quarters, so you're applying only about a teaspoon or so of fertilizer per watering. This may sound like a lot of work, but wait until you see the results. Bloom city!

If fertilizing every time you water is too much hassle for you, use a liquid fertilizer once every week or two. Follow the rates recommended on the label. Your annuals will still do great.

Using Organic Fertilizers

Organic fertilizers come in all shapes and sizes. These days, there are as many definitions of *organic* as there are cappuccino stands in Seattle. Basically, anything that was once alive (such as seaweed or cows) or was produced by a living thing is considered organic. Some widely accepted organic fertilizers include manure, compost, fish emulsion, bonemeal, and greensand.

Manure from horses, cows, and poultry is the most common organic source of nitrogen. The salts in fresh manure can burn plants, so you must make sure that the manure has aged for a while or is completely composted before you apply it. Many gardeners work manure into the soil in the fall and then wait until spring to plant. This approach allows plenty of time for the manure to "mellow."

Bonemeal is a good organic source of phosphorus, but once in the ground, it takes a long time to break down into a form that plants can use. Greensand, a naturally occurring rock mineral found mostly in New Jersey, is an excellent organic source of potassium and also includes many micronutrients.

Many people today prefer to use organic fertilizer because they feel that it's better for their plants. The truth is that your annuals don't know whether the nutrients they're getting have organic or synthetic sources. But organic fertilizers do have an advantage in that, besides providing nutrients, they also add bulk to the soil and improve its structure in ways that synthetic fertilizers cannot.

Organic fertilizers are better for the environment because they support soil-building earthworms and microbes and because they are usually recycled — not manufactured — materials. However, organic fertilizers are often difficult to handle, their nutrient contents are unpredictable, and the nutrients they do contain aren't always immediately available to the plant. They tend to be higher priced, but if you're creative, you can make your own through composting or gathering aged manure from local farms.

You can supply all the nutrients that annuals need by using only organic materials, but you must take some care and effort to ensure that sufficient amounts of nitrogen, phosphorus, and potassium are available to plants throughout the season. You have to observe your plants carefully, noting their vigor and general color, and then add more or less fertilizer with each application until you get the results you want.

Table 9-1 lists some common organic fertilizers, their average nutrient analysis, and moderate rates at which you can apply them. Because nutrient contents of organic fertilizers can vary greatly, use less if you have doubts.

Before applying bonemeal or any other dusty fertilizer, get a good dust mask. Just because a fertilizer is organic doesn't mean that it can't harm you.

Table 9-1	Common Organic Fertilizers	
Organic Fertilizer	*Average Nutrient Analysis*	*Application Rate per 100 Square Feet*
Blood meal	10-0-0	2 pounds
Bonemeal (steamed)	1-11-0	2 pounds
Cow manure	2-2-2	10 to 15 pounds
Fish emulsion	4-1-1	15 to 20 gallons (1 tablespoon per gallon)
Greensand	0-0-7	5 pounds
Horse manure	2-1-2	10 to 15 pounds
Poultry manure	4-4-2	5 pounds

Chapter 10

Pruning, Deadheading, and Other Joys of Gardening

. . . .

In This Chapter

▶ Choosing the right tools

▶ Deadheading faded flowers

▶ Staking slumping annuals

▶ Pruning and pinching

▶ Mulching the right way

. . . .

*Y*ou can view your routine gardening chores as, well, work, or you can view them as opportunities. I recommend the second approach: Deadheading flowers can be an opportunity to visit with your neighbors; pruning the petunias gives you a temporary escape from your teenager's hip-hop music; and spreading mulch offers an excuse to enjoy the beauty of nature.

No matter how you view your gardening chores, the payoff is worth your time and effort. By protecting the investment you've made in your annuals, you get a garden that looks good for the long term. Conscientious gardeners are rewarded with prettier, healthier plants that last longer and provide a most impressive display.

This chapter shows you how to efficiently deadhead, stake, pinch, prune, mulch, and do a few wrap-up jobs. It also explains the basic tools and materials that you need to maintain a healthy garden. Use the information in this chapter to keep your annuals in the best shape possible. (Unfortunately, annuals sometimes demand other kinds of care, including pest and weed control, which I cover in Chapters 11 and 12.)

Tackling Key Gardening Tasks

Garden maintenance involves four simple tasks:

- ✓ **Deadheading:** Removing faded flowers to stimulate new flower production

- ✓ **Staking:** Providing support to stems and blossoms that may otherwise fall over or snap

- ✓ **Pinching and pruning:** Removing parts of the plant to control growth, maximize flower production, and give plants good form

- ✓ **Mulching:** Covering the soil around the plants to keep moisture in and weeds out

Depending on how you approach these chores, you can either slave away for endless hours or get the jobs done quickly and efficiently. Timing is important to help you keep the tasks small and manageable, not large and overwhelming. Here are some key strategies for garden maintenance:

- ✓ **Start the jobs early, before the situation gets out of hand.** This is the most important bit of advice for your garden maintenance. Anyone who has attempted to cut back a jungle of wild and woolly flowers or struggled to upright drooping 4-foot-flower stems can testify that heeding this advice saves you time and toil later. Doing your gardening jobs early makes them significantly smaller and more manageable.

- ✓ **Always do jobs as you notice that they need to be done.** If you head out to the garden to snip a few flowers or pinch back a leggy stem, be on the lookout for faded blossoms to deadhead, debris to clean up, or floppy stems to support. Doing multiple jobs at once is a simple time-saver.

- ✓ **Observe a regular maintenance schedule.** By so doing, you ensure that no chore gets too far out of hand. For example, try to weed and deadhead your flower beds weekly. That doesn't mean spending all day Saturday weeding; it just means that each section of your garden gets attention at least once a week. For example, if you weed and deadhead a small patch of your garden for a half hour every weekday evening, you may be able to cover the entire area over the course of five days. That leaves you Saturday and Sunday to enjoy your handiwork.

✔ **Be a bucket gardener.** Hide a plastic bucket near your garden (or take one with you when you go) so that, as you pinch a stem or snap off a flower, you have an easy and convenient place to toss your garden waste until you can take it to the compost pile. For large areas, consider keeping a plastic garbage container (the kind with wheels is great) or a wheelbarrow nearby. Keeping equipment handy means that you are more likely to spend a few minutes doing chores each time you visit the garden rather than waiting until you have a large chunk of time to lug all your equipment from a distant spot.

✔ **Make regular tours of the garden.** Think of these tours as mini-vacations — time away from your kitchen, computer, or laundry room. Don't get your hands dirty on these garden strolls, but do make a mental note of what jobs you need to tackle next. When the time comes to do some work in the garden, you already know what tools you need and what chores are most pressing, so you can work smarter.

✔ **Make sure that you have the materials and tools you need to do the job.** Store tools in a set location where you can always find them, and keep them clean. Keep track of supplies such as stakes, ties, and mulch and restock as amounts get low; don't wait until they're completely gone. I describe the tools you need and how to care for them in the upcoming section "Using the Right Tool for the Right Job."

✔ **Evaluate how much maintenance you're doing.** Is it manageable, or is it taking a toll on you? If it seems that you're spending too much time and effort on your garden, ask yourself whether you could be doing your chores more efficiently to save time. If not, consider scaling down the garden to a size that you can more easily handle.

Using the Right Tool for the Right Job

To do any job right, you need the right tools; gardening is no exception. Fortunately, with a well-planned and properly

planted annual bed, you can perform most garden maintenance jobs with a minimum of tools and materials.

Seven essential tools for growing annuals

You need some key tools for maintaining and planting annuals. The good news is that you may already have some of
these tools, and because the digging won't have to be very
deep, you don't have to get into the "heavy metal."

Make sure you have the following tools:

- ✔ **Garden spade or shovel:** This is the single most important tool for digging, loosening, turning, amending, and
  spreading everything from soil to compost to manure.
  You have a lot of choices from a size, price, and quality
  standpoint. Choose a tool that feels right in both weight
  and length. Some people prefer a shovel or spade with a
  long, straight handle; others prefer one with a shorter
  handle and plastic or metal grip. Mimic the motion you'll
  use to shovel, and find the size that's most comfortable
  for you. Remember to pay for quality if you want to
  invest in a lasting tool.

- ✔ **Steel bow rake:** This rake is the one with the stiff tines.
  It's a must-have tool for spreading, leveling, or removing
  rocks and debris. A steel bow rake helps you break up
  clods, and when you turn the rake over, the back edge is
  excellent for leveling and smoothing a seed bed.

- ✔ **Hand trowel:** This handheld tool is important for digging
  small holes for planting seedlings or transplants from six-
  packs or 4-inch containers. It's also handy for popping
  out weeds and removing small rocks. A thick-bladed
  farmer's or gardener's knife is an acceptable substitute.
  These knives have a wide, sturdy blade and are the best
  for solid digging; they don't bend the way some trowels
  do. Choose a tool that is the right weight for you and has
  a comfortable handle.

- ✔ **Hoe:** Try a scuffle hoe for a more efficient tool than the
  basic bladed hoe. Compared to an old-fashioned hoe,
  scuffle hoes work with a push/pull action that cuts off or
  digs out small weeds right at the soil surface. This tool is

good for working between plants and on hard, compacted surfaces such as paths.

✔ **Leaf rake:** Small rakes — about 8 inches wide — are ideal for work in close quarters; large rakes are handy for removing and collecting light debris and, you guessed it, leaves. The tines of a rake may be made of bamboo, plastic, or flexible metal. Consider investing in an expandable rake, which allows you to expand or contract the tines, changing the width so that you can use it over large areas or between plants in a bed.

✔ **Pruners:** No gardener can live without a pair of pruners. Use this hand-held cutting tool for snipping stems up to ¾-inch diameter or so. Pruners come in handy when you're cutting flowers, pruning plants to improve their shape, or clipping mature plants after they're finished blooming. Pruners are available in a wide price range and several styles. High-quality pruners give you clean cuts with a minimum of effort and will last for years. Look for comfort and sharp blades.

✔ **Garden cart:** Carts are lightweight and stable, allowing you to haul loads of heavy stuff, including soil, compost, or mulch. Let a cart do the work when you need to transport your plants to the garden. It can handle flats of flowers or 1-gallon pots. Look for a cart with four wheels set close together for easy maneuvering through tight spaces. Or if you prefer, you can use a wheelbarrow.

Nonessential but handy garden supplies

If you can afford a few extra gardening goodies, add the following items to your shopping list:

✔ **Garden gloves:** Choose cloth if don't want to spend a bunch; try sheepskin or pigskin for long-lasting protection.

✔ **Water wand:** This gadget is an aluminum pipe that attaches to the end of the hose and produces a gentle shower that's perfect for seeds and seedlings.

✔ **Soft ties:** Garden centers sell various plastic tapes and twist ties for tying stems to stakes and vines to trellises.

You can also use regular jute twine, or even strips of soft fabric.

✔ **Hose guide:** This device keeps hoses outside low beds so that you don't pull the hose over small plants. Use a guide to protect plants along curves or corners.

✔ **Pronged weeder:** This little tool (about a foot long) is great, especially if you don't have a gardener's knife. One end has a small hoelike blade, and the other end has a dual-pronged point that's perfect for those nasty weeds and general light cultivation.

Deadheading: Out with the Old

Avoiding all cheap-shot jokes about touring rock bands, I will simply say that *deadheading* is the act of cutting or pinching off a faded flower. It's an important job: By removing the spent flower, you stimulate the plant to produce a new bud in its exhaustive quest to make seeds to reproduce. Deadheading not only keeps plants looking tidy, but it also prolongs the bloom period and gives you significantly more flowers.

Start deadheading as soon as you see the flowers fade and the petals begin to fall off. Remove part of the stem as well as the faded flower, so that you're sure to get the seed pod, too. With some flowers, such as petunias, you can pull off the petal part and think you've done the job, but the seed pod remains. Use your fingers, as shown in Figure 10-1, to pinch off flowers with fleshy stems. (Marigolds make a particularly satisfying snap.) Use pruners for stiffer or more stubborn flowers.

Watch for flower-producing side shoots a bit down on the stem. When removing spent flowers, cut the stem above this point to save the new buds coming on. Cosmos, zinnia, and gloriosa daisy are famous for producing these lower buds. If you don't see any side shoots, cut the stem just above a set of leaves.

Figure 10-1: Removing dead blooms coaxes your annuals into producing new blooms.

Offering Some Support: Basics of Staking

Staking is a simple but important job — especially for plants more than 3 feet tall and for plants with large, heavy flowers or slender stems. Staking keeps plants steady in the wind and ensures that blossoms stay healthy and upright. It gives the garden a neat and tidy look and helps plants produce the maximum number of flowers.

You almost always have to stake tall annuals, such as cosmos, sunflowers, spider flowers, salpiglossis, nicotiana, larkspur, gloriosa daisy, cornflower, and globe amaranthus. You also may need to stake certain tall varieties of zinnia, dahlia, and snapdragon. Keep an eye on all your annuals as they develop to see whether flowers seem to be giving in to gravity, thus requiring you to stake them.

Stake early! You'll have far better results if you put the stake in when you set out transplants or after seedlings reach a few inches tall. By staking early, you can direct the stems to grow upward right from the start and tie them at intervals along the stake as they grow. After a mass of flowers falls over, it's difficult to bring them back to a vertical postion without damaging them. Don't worry about the aethetics of the stake; although the stake may look stark at first, the stems and leaves will quickly surround the stake and hide it from view.

Tie stems to slender bamboo sticks, wooden stakes, or even straight and sturdy woody branches that you saved from your pruning chores. For light plants with sturdy stems, such as cosmos and cornflower, you can use twine or twist ties. For large-flowered plants, such as sunflowers, use plastic garden tape or strips of fabric — under the weight of those heavy flowers, twine can cut into stem tissue. For the largest plants, insert a single stake a few inches from the stem at planting time and loosely tie the seedling to the stake. As the plant grows, continue to tie the stem at intervals along the stake, as shown on the left plant in Figure 10-2.

You can also corral smaller plants by setting stakes in the ground around the circumference and winding ties or twine horizontally to enclose the area. Or you can buy wire stakes with a loop that encircles individual stems (shown on the right-hand plant in Figure 10-2). Also available are mini-fences that hook together in sections to support many plants at once.

Don't forget to stake your container plants. Stake these flowers when they're little by using either one slender stake per plant (pushed several inches down), or three or four stakes around the edge of pot with twine wrapped around the them. Try green wire stakes in containers — they blend in and disappear among the flowers.

If you're growing annual climbers (such as sweet pea, morning glory, scarlet runner bean, and so on), be sure to plant seeds where the flowers will have serious support nearby. Good choices are planting areas near a fence, lattice, post, pillar, or arbor. Many of these climbers twine themselves around the support, but you may need to give some stems guidance by using soft ties. Insert U-shaped staples in posts, pillars, or fence boards to run the ties through.

Figure 10-2: Staking a single large plant or corralling many stems.

Pruning and Pinching: It Hurts You More Than It Hurts the Plant

Pinching and pruning annuals are far simpler tasks than similar care for more permanent plants, such as perennials and shrubs. Still, the jobs clearly have their rewards.

Pinching refers to removal of soft tip growth and is usually done with the thumb and forefinger. It encourages plants to become bushy and full rather than rangy and tall. A side effect of pinching is that plants develop uniform growth and plenty of buds — although pinching tends to postpone the flowers a bit if you remove their buds.

Pinch plants when they're young — before they develop long stems. Remove the tip growth by pinching above a set of leaves. To promote good overall shape, pinch both upright and side stems (as shown in Figure 10-3). When you have a mass of plants in the bed, pinch back the tallest ones so that they don't shoot up past their neighbors. Good candidates for pinching include petunias, snapdragons, impatiens, chrysanthemums, marguerites, and geraniums. Avoid pinching plants that send up strong central shoots with flowers at the tip, such as stock and celosia. These flowers don't branch well anyway, so you don't want to pinch off all the flower buds.

Figure 10-3: Pinching promotes a fuller, more compact plant.

Pruning is the process of cutting back plants to keep them within the boundaries you've set and to promote bushier growth. Annuals rarely need the heavy-duty pruning that perennials and shrubs demand. Trim stems that are rangy, floppy, or sprawling onto neighboring flowers; trim as often as necessary to keep them under control. Make cuts just above a set of leaves or side shoot. This technique promotes both bushiness and new buds. After the first round of blooms, especially if you haven't deadheaded, you can try giving plants an overall trimming to encourage a new round of blooms.

So which annuals require serious pruning? You probably need to worry only about globe amaranthus, four o'clocks, felicia, and some types of petunia, especially cascading or trailing varieties that become very leggy.

Mulching Miracles

A mulch is simply a soil cover. Mulching an annual garden cuts down on the amount of water needed and helps control weeds. The principle is simple: The soil is cooled and protected by the application of a top layer of some type of material. You can use compost, leaf mold, crushed stone, or bark, or you can use inorganic materials, such as landscape fabric, plastic sheeting, or even newspapers. As long as the material is attractive, you'll have a neat-looking garden, to boot. A layer of mulch also helps hide drip irrigation tubes (which I discuss in Chapter 8).

Try this trio of quick and easy steps for mulching the annuals in your garden:

1. **Select a mulch material.**

   What do you have on hand that can be used as mulch? Compost or perhaps the by-products of chopped, shredded stuff from a chipper/shredder machine? You also can purchase packaged mulches in bulk or bags; redwood shavings, bark (in small, medium, and coarse chunks or shredded), cocoa or rice hulls, and compost are sold this way.

   Generally the finer the material, the better it looks with your annuals. Plastic sheeting, landscape fabric, or old newspapers are okay, but they really are ugly and better used in vegetable gardens, where appearance matters less. If you do use an unsightly mulch, you can cover it with a layer of bark, compost, or crushed stone.

2. **Spread your mulch material around annuals but leave a few inches of bare earth around the base of each annual.**

   This technique provides a little reservoir for water and keeps plant stems from rotting or becoming diseased. In general, annuals like a 2- to 3-inch layer of mulch; the thicker the mulch, the fewer weeds. If you use a layer of newspapers or landscape fabric first, you need less mulch on top — just enough to cover. Because these are not permanent plants, you don't need anything much thicker.

3. **Make periodic inspections of the garden to see that mulch stays put.**

   Marauding pets, wind, water, and even tiny garden visitors like mice and squirrels can easily displace this soil covering. Keep extra mulch on hand so that you can always add mulch when and where you need it.

To find out more about mulch, turn to Chapter 11.

Chapter 11

Weed Wars and Your Ally, Mulch

In This Chapter

▶ Controlling weeds before you plant
▶ Reducing weeds after you plant
▶ Letting mulches do the work
▶ Deciding what type of mulch to use
▶ Knowing when to mulch

*W*eeds and mulches in the same chapter? Well, why not? In the eternal battle against weeds — those aggressive, moisture-stealing plants that always show up where you least want them — mulches can be one of your most valuable weapons.

Outwitting Weeds

A weed is any plant growing where you don't want it to. Some weeds are worse than others, but in general, gardeners don't want any weeds in their flower beds. Weeds compete with annuals for light, water, and nutrients, resulting in weaker annuals. And weeds make your flower bed look messy.

Luckily, weeds are easier to control in plantings of annual flowers than they are in other garden situations. Pulling out annuals at the end of the season gives you the perfect chance to deal with weeds in an open area and to treat them more aggressively so that they'll never dare to return. In addition, if you grow annuals close together — jowl-to-jowl, so to speak — the flowers can shade the weeds and cause them to die from lack of light.

Before you plant

You can reduce weeds in your annual flower beds in many ways and at many points in the gardening process. Here's what you can do before planting, at the end or beginning of the season, or whenever your beds are empty:

- **Presprout weed seeds:** This technique really cuts down on the number of weeds that come up from seeds. Prepare the planting bed several weeks before it's time to plant. Make sure that the soil is nice and level and ready to go, as I describe in Chapter 6. Then water the soil well and wait for a few days. Presto, young weeds sprout.

  You can kill these weeds in one of three ways: Pull them by hand, rake the bed lightly to uproot the seedlings and let them dry out to die, or spray them with an herbicide such as glyphosate (sold under a number of brand names). As much as you may oppose the use of herbicides, they do kill the toughest weeds. No matter how you get rid of the young weeds, try to disturb the soil as little as possible — or else you'll simply bring more seeds to the surface, and you'll need to start your eradication process all over again.

- **Solarize the soil:** This technique, which uses power from the sun to kill weeds, works best in the middle of summer in climates that get very hot, like the southwestern United States. Check with your local cooperative extension service to see how effective solarization is in your area.

  The process does take a while (at least six weeks). Prepare the bed for planting and water it well. Dig a 6- to 12-inch-deep trench around the perimeter. Cover the entire area with thick (4 ml), clear plastic sheeting, place the edges of the plastic in the trenches, and fill the trenches with soil. Then wait. The temperatures underneath can become hot enough to kill insects, disease organisms, and weeds.

- **Apply a pre-emergence herbicide:** Pre-emergence herbicides kill seedlings before they can reach the soil surface — after they sprout and before they emerge from the soil. Both liquid and granular forms are available. Apply a pre-emergence herbicide before planting or after annuals are growing; either way, water the ground thoroughly after the application. In addition to weed seeds, the seeds of annual flowers also feel the effects of this herbicide, so don't use pre-emergence herbicides if you plan to sow flower seeds in the bed. After applying a pre-emergence herbicide, you can safely set out trans-plants; read the product label carefully and follow instruc-tions exactly. How long pre-emergence herbicides remain effective varies by product.

Think carefully before using a pre-emergence herbicide; it may adversely affect what you can grow in the same spot later. For example, after you use such an herbicide on an area, you may not be able to sow seeds there for quite a while. And you probably don't want to grow vegetables there for even longer — food crops and herbicides are not a good mix in home gardens.

After you plant

When annuals are already growing in a bed, here are the approaches you can take to get rid of weeds:

- ✔ **Pull weeds out by hand:** Get them while they're young, and they'll come out of the ground easily. Remove the roots, too.

- ✔ **Cultivate:** Simply hoeing or lightly turning the soil between annuals exposes the roots of the weeds and kills many of them. The technique is most effective if you do it often and when the weeds are small. Some cultivating tools, such as three-pronged hand cultivators or special-purpose hoes, are designed especially for this purpose, but a regular hoe or trowel does the trick, too.

- ✔ **Spot-spray with herbicide:** You can use weed killers such as glyphosate, which affects weeds after they're growing, to spot-spray tough weeds. But be aware that if you spray any herbicides on your annuals, they'll die, too. Sometimes, you can use a piece of cardboard or a sheet of plastic to protect nearby plants from herbicides that you're spraying on weeds. Or you can put a bottomless box or tin can over a weed before you spray it. Read the entire product label and follow instructions exactly.

- ✔ **Mulch:** Mulching is an important weapon in the war against weeds. See the section "Thank You Very Mulch," later in this chapter.

Battling really tough weeds

Some perennial weeds (those that live year to year) can really be troublesome. At the top of that list are Bermuda grass (in mild-winter areas) and bindweed (almost anywhere).

Bermuda grass spreads vigorously by nasty wiry stems. The underground stems are called rhizomes; the above-ground stems are called stolons. Bermuda grass also produces a ton of seeds, which is another way that it spreads. This monster just spreads and spreads and then spreads some more. That feature makes Bermuda grass desirable for a good lawn, but in flower beds, it's nothing but trouble.

Bindweed, sometimes called wild morning glory, is a rampantly spreading vine that sprawls over and around annuals. You can recognize it by its small, round, white flowers and sword-shaped leaves. If you try pulling it out, it breaks off at ground level and returns the next day. (At least it seems that way.) Bindweed also produces a ton of seeds.

Both of these weeds require persistence to control:

- ✔ Pull seedlings as soon as you see them. Use a trowel or weeding tool to make sure that you remove all the roots.

- ✔ Spot treat with glyphosate as I describe elsewhere in this chapter. Bermuda grass is easiest to kill when its whirlybird-like seedheads appear. But even then, you may have to spray twice. A few herbicides are available that specifically kill grasses but won't hurt your annuals. Ask your nursery expert to recommend one.

- ✔ When you work the soil in the spring or fall, remove the clumps of Bermuda grass roots. You'll never uproot them all, but whatever you can do will help.

Thank You Very Mulch

Any material that you place over the surface of the soil, usually right over the root zone of growing plants, is considered a mulch. Mulches offer many benefits to annuals:

✔ They conserve water by reducing soil temperatures and evaporation. The idea is to keep the soil cool by buffering direct sunlight.

✔ They prevent wild fluctuations in soil-moisture levels that can really spell disaster in hot weather.

✔ They smother weed seeds and prevent them from germinating.

✔ Any weeds that come up in a loose mulch are easy to pull.

✔ As mulches break down, they add nutrients and improve the texture of the soil.

✔ Mulches look good and give the ground a tidy and clean appearance.

Choosing your mulch

The two basic kinds of mulch are organic and inorganic. For flower growers, organic mulches are by far more useful. They look at home with the informal quality of annuals and also help improve planting bed soils.

Organic mulches include grass clippings, compost, wood chips, leaf mold, pine needles, shredded bark, nut shells, cotton gin waste, straw, grain and fruit by-products, composted manure, mushroom compost, peat moss, sawdust, and even newspapers. Some are easier to find in different parts of the country.

Certain organic mulches come with caveats:

✔ Bark mulches, such as pine needles, are quite acidic. If you use them, keep a close eye on the soil pH and correct it accordingly. (See Chapter 6 for more information about soil pH.)

✔ Grass clippings decay quickly and must be replenished often. But that's okay, because there are usually more grass clippings where the first batch came from. Make sure that the grass hasn't gone to seed before you cut it; otherwise, you may have a lawn coming up in your flower bed. Also, be sure that no herbicides (weed killers) have been used on your lawn, because the residue can damage or kill annuals.

✔ Some organic mulches, such as fresh sawdust, rob your soil of nitrogen as they break down. Counteract this effect by adding supplemental nitrogen to your annuals if they are mysteriously growing slowly or starting to turn yellow.

✔ Peat moss can become hard and crusty when exposed to weather. Water may not penetrate it, so the water runs off instead of soaking in to the roots. Try to avoid peat moss or mix it with something else — it's so darn expensive anyway.

✔ Some lightweight mulches, such as straw or cocoa hulls, can blow around in the wind. You may want to avoid them if you live in a windy area.

✔ Types of composted manure vary in the amount of nitrogen they contain. If you use them by themselves as a mulch, you run the risk of burning your annuals. If you want to mulch with manure, mix the manure with three times the volume of another organic mulch before applying.

You can purchase organic mulches, such as shredded bark, compost, and leaf mold, in bags, or sometimes in bulk, from nurseries and garden centers. Grass clippings, compost, and wood chips come free from your yard and garden.

Gardeners usually don't use inorganic mulches, such as stone and plastic, in annual flower beds. However, you may want to use products called landscape fabrics in your garden. Landscape fabrics, available at many nurseries and garden centers, are made of permeable material that you spread on the ground before planting. You cut little X-shaped holes in the fabric and plant through the holes, as shown in Figure 11-1. The fabrics block weed growth just as an organic mulch does, but you can roll up the fabrics at the end of the season and use them again next year. Some organic landscape fabrics that naturally break down at the end of the year are also now available.

Laying it down

Most of the time, a 2- to 3-inch layer of mulch spread evenly beneath the plants is plenty. However, you may have to replenish it during the growing season because many organic mulches break down quickly. Plan on replenishing when the layer thins out or, worse yet, when you see weeds coming through it.

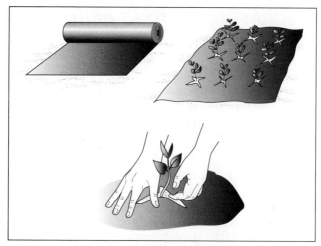

Figure 11-1: Unroll landscape fabric over your flower beds and cut holes and X-shaped slits for your plants to poke through.

Don't spread mulch all the way to the stem of the plant. Leave several inches of breathing (and drinking!) room for your growing plant. Figure 11-2 shows an example of a well-mulched annual.

Figure 11-2: Always leave the space immediately surrounding the plant stem free of mulch and debris.

Knowing when to mulch

Your mulching schedule really depends on the type of annuals you grow and when you plant them.

- **Cool-season annuals planted in early spring:** Pansies and other annuals that do well in cool spring weather will benefit from extra warmth early in the season, when it's a little too cool for cool-season annuals to really thrive. Don't mulch at this point; instead, let the sun hit the soil directly and warm it up. Later on, when the weather starts to get too hot for cool-season annuals, cool things off by mulching. So wait to mulch until after the soil starts to warm and the plants need regular water. As the days heat up, mulch helps the plants thrive and bloom longer into hot weather.

- **Cool-season annuals planted in late summer or early fall:** For these plants, you want a cooling effect during hot weather, so spread the mulch right after planting. When the weather starts to cool, rake off or remove the mulch so that the soil can warm. Removing the mulch prolongs the bloom longer into the winter. If you really want to go all-out and try to get some of your hardier annuals through the winter so that they bloom very early the following spring, mulch again after the ground starts to freeze. This mulching schedule helps prevent the soil from repeated freezing and thawing, which can literally rip some plants right out of the ground.

- **Warm-season annuals planted in spring:** You may want to keep the ground clear if you are planting really early — the more heat the better. Otherwise, mulch at planting time.

Chapter 12

Outsmarting Pests and Diseases

*M*any gardeners, especially beginners, are surprised to find out just how many pest and disease problems that they can actually prevent or avoid. The more you know about the plants you grow, the pests that are common to them, the types of pest control measures available, and how to protect the diversity of life that occupies your garden, the less likely it is that you'll have to take drastic measures, such as using strong chemicals.

The following common-sense pest and disease prevention tips are your first line of defense:

✔ **Plant in the right location.** Many pests become more troublesome when annuals are grown in less-than-ideal conditions. For example, when sun-loving annuals are grown in shade, mildew problems often become more severe.

✔ **Grow healthy plants.** Healthy plants are less likely to develop problems. Prepare the soil properly before planting and avoid overfertilizing and overwatering.

✔ **Choose resistant plants.** If you know that a certain disease is common in your area, choose plants that are not susceptible or that resist infection to it. Some varieties of annuals are resistant to specific diseases. Look for disease-resistance information in seed catalogs and nursery descriptions.

✔ **Keep your garden clean.** Cleaning up spent plants, weeds, and other garden debris can eliminate hiding places for many pests.

✔ **Rotate your annuals.** Avoid planting the same annuals in the same location year after year. Rotation prevents pests and diseases specific to certain annuals from building up in your soil.

✔ **Know the enemy.** The more you know about specific pests and diseases common to your area — when they occur and how they spread — the more easily you can avoid them.

When Bad Bugs Happen to Nice Gardens

Actually, bugs are neither bad nor good. They just do what they're programmed to do: eat, grow, and reproduce. The problem comes in when bugs and gardeners want to enjoy the same flowers. A little conflict of interest, you might say!

An errant grasshopper may not be cause for concern, but if that same grasshopper brings along his brothers, sisters, and cousins to join in on the zinnia feast at your expense, he becomes a pest. When you start seeing a number of the same type of insects, such as aphids, in your garden, and you notice that their activity is focused on certain plants, such as cosmos, then you need to act quickly and decisively.

Insects that prey on annuals

Here are the most common insect pests that you are likely to find infesting your annuals and the best way to control them:

✔ **Aphids:** These tiny, pear-shaped pests (shown in Figure 12-1) come in many colors, including black, green, and red. They congregate on new growth and flower buds, sucking plant sap with their needlelike noses. Heavy infestations can cause distorted growth and weaken plants. Vinca and cosmos are two annuals that aphids commonly attack. Aphids leave behind a sticky sap that may turn black with sooty mold.

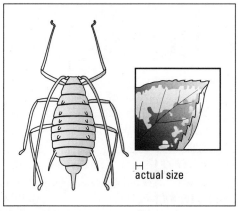

H
actual size

Figure 12-1: Aphids weaken plants, but they're easy to control.

Aphids are easy to control. You can knock them off sturdy plants with a strong jet of water from a hose, or you can use insecticidal soap or pyrethrins, described in the section "Botanical insecticides." The soap helps wash off the sooty mold (the harmless black gunk that comes with aphids). But usually if you just wait a week or two, the aphid population boom is followed by a buildup of beneficial insects, especially lady beetles, who usually take matters into their own hands before serious damage occurs.

✔ **Geranium budworms:** These frustrating pests (shown in Figure 12-2) love geraniums, nicotiana, ageratum, and petunias. The small caterpillars bore into flower buds and eat the flowers before they open, or they simply feed on open blooms. The result is no flowers, only leaves. Not a pretty sight!

To confirm the presence of these heartless monsters, look for small holes in geranium blossoms or the tiny black droppings that the caterpillars leave behind. You may also see the worms on the flowers. To control, pick off infested geranium buds and spray with Bt. Bt is a naturally occurring bacteria that parasitizes the budworm. It's the most environmentally-friendly pesticide to use, but chemical-based pesticides (such as pyrethrins, carbaryl, and acephate) also work. All are available at local garden centers and are registered for home gardener use.

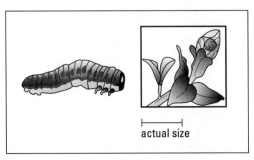

actual size

Figure 12-2: Geranium budworms like to feast on petunias as well as geraniums.

✔ **Japanese beetles:** Especially troublesome east of the Mississippi River, these pests feed on both flowers and foliage, often skeletonizing leaves. They particularly love zinnias and marigolds. Shown in Figure 12-3, Japanese beetles are about ½ inch long and have coppery bodies and metallic green heads.

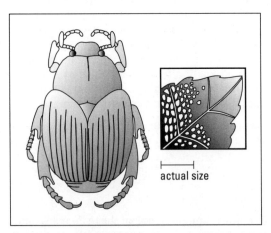

actual size

Figure 12-3: Japanese beetles are especially fond of zinnias and marigolds.

Controlling this pest can be tough. Treating your lawn and garden soil with parasitic nematodes or milky spore (a form of Bt) may reduce the white C-shaped larvae, but more adults will probably fly in from your neighbor's yard. Turning the soil to expose the grubs to birds also may help. Floral-scented traps that attract adult beetles are available, but the traps may attract more beetles than you had before. If you try the traps, keep them at least 100 feet from your flowers.

Neem, insecticidal soap, and pyrethrins are effective against adult beetles. Traditional chemicals that may help include carbaryl and acephate. You also can simply pick the beetles off your flowers and stomp on them.

✔ **Cutworms:** These ½-inch-long, grayish caterpillars (shown in Figure 12-4) emerge during spring and early summer nights to eat the stems of young seedling stems, causing them to fall over like small timbers.

They also move on to older plants and feed on leaves and flowers.

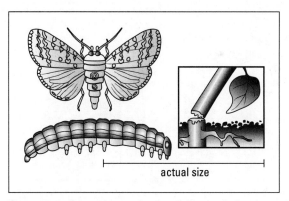

actual size

Figure 12-4: Cutworms can do a lot of damage before sprouting wings and flying off.

To protect seedlings, surround their stems with a barrier that prevents the cutworms from crawling close and feeding. These contraptions can be as simple as an empty cardboard toilet-paper roll, a Styrofoam cup with the bottom cut out, or a collar made from aluminum foil — just make sure that the barrier encircles the stem completely and is set 1 inch deep in the soil. You can also trap cutworms by leaving boards around the garden. The

worms will hide under the boards during the day, giving
you the chance to collect and destroy them. Parasitic
nematodes are also effective against cutworms.

✔ **Snails and slugs:** These soft-bodied mollusks feed on
tender leaves and flowers during the cool of the night or
during rainy weather. Snails have shells; slugs don't. (See
Figure 12-5.) Both proliferate in damp areas, hiding under
boards, mulch, and other garden debris.

To control these pests, you can roam the garden at night
with a flashlight and play pick-and-stomp. Or you can
trap them with saucers of beer — these guys can't resist
a brewski, even if it means drowning to death. Bury a cat-
food can, cup, or dish so that the rim is at ground level,
and refill regularly. Snails and slugs do not cross copper,
so you can also surround raised beds with a thin copper
stripping sold in most nurseries. In southern California,
you can release decollate snails, which prey on pest
snails. Ask your cooperative extension office for information. If all else fails, you can use poison snail bait.

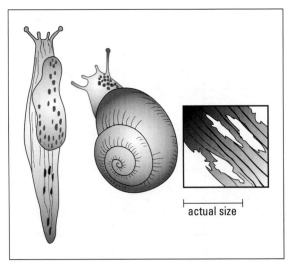

actual size

Figure 12-5: Slugs and snails like to hide in damp areas.

✔ **Spider mites:** These tiny arachnids can barely be seen
without a magnifying glass. If the population gets big
enough, you can see their fine webbing beneath the
leaves. (See Figure 12-6.) And as they suck plant juices,

the leaves become yellowish, with silvery stippling or sheen. If things get really bad, the plant may start dropping leaves. Mites are most common in hot, dry summer climates and on dusty plants. Marigolds and columbines are commonly infested.

A daily bath with a strong jet of water from a hose helps keep infestations down. You can control spider mites with insecticidal soap, which also helps to clean off the plants' leaves. Summer oil is also effective, as is releasing predatory mites.

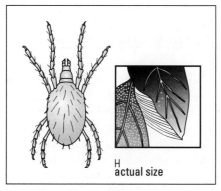

H
actual size

Figure 12-6: Spider mites are too tiny to identify by sight, but their damage is unmistakable.

✔ **Thrips:** Another nearly invisible troublemaker, thrips (see Figure 12-7) feed on flower petals, causing them to be discolored and the buds to be deformed as they open. Thrips also feed on leaves, giving the foliage a deformed and stippled look. (You can distinguish thrips from spider mites by the small fecal pellets that thrips leave behind.) Impatiens and many other annuals can become targets of thrips.

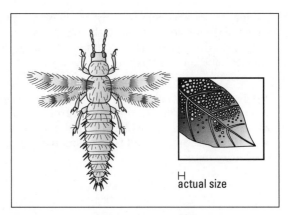

H
actual size

Figure 12-7: Thrips damage flower petals and leaves.

Many beneficial insects feed on thrips, especially lacewings. Insecticidal soaps are also effective, as are several stronger insecticides, including acephate.

✔ **Whiteflies:** Looking like small white gnats, whiteflies (see Figure 12-8) suck plant juices and can proliferate in warm climates and greenhouses. They tend to congregate on the undersides of leaves. You can trap whiteflies with yellow sticky traps sold in nurseries. In greenhouses, you can release Encarsia wasps, which prey on greenhouse whiteflies. Insecticidal soaps, summer oil, and pyrethrins are effective sprays.

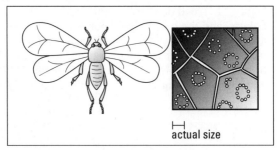

H
actual size

Figure 12-8: Whiteflies gather on undersides of leaves.

Fighting back

If pests begin to bother your garden in serious ways and you need to take further action, start with the first line of defense: pesticides that are effective against a particular pest, that are relatively safe to use, and that have a mild impact on the rest of your garden's life forms.

In general, these products are short-lived after you use them in the garden — that's what makes them so good. However, in order to get effective control, you often must use them more frequently than stronger chemicals.

Biological controls

Biological controls involve pitting one living thing against another, such as beneficial insects against harmful insects. Beneficial insects are the good soldiers of your garden — the insects that feed on the bugs that bother your annuals. You probably already have many different kinds of beneficial insects in your garden, but you also can purchase them at garden suppliers and release them into your garden. The more beneficial bugs, the fewer pests.

You can purchase the following beneficial insects to help control the pests that are dining on your annuals:

- ✔ **Lady beetles:** These are basic ladybugs. Both the orange-red adult beetles and the lizardlike larvae are especially good at feeding on small insects such as aphids and thrips. Releasing adult beetles is sometimes not very effective because Mother Nature has preprogrammed them to migrate on down the road, so they leave your garden quickly. Try preconditioned lady beetles, which have been deprogrammed (you don't want to know how); they are more likely to stick around. And release them just before sundown. That way, they'll at least spend the night. Release a few thousand of them in spring, as soon as you notice the first aphid.

- ✔ **Green lacewings:** Their voracious larvae feed on aphids, mites, thrips, and various insect eggs. These insects are among the most effective for garden use. Release them in your garden in late spring, after the danger of frost has passed.

✔ **Parasitic nematodes:** These microscopic worms parasitize many types of soil-dwelling and burrowing insects, including cutworms and grubs of Japanese beetles. Because grubs usually inhabit lawns, you have to apply these worms there, too, as well as around the base of your plants. Apply parasitic nematodes to the soil around the base of your plants once in the spring.

✔ **Predatory mites:** These tiny creatures feed on spider mites and thrips. Add them to your garden in the spring, as soon as frost danger has passed.

✔ **Trichogramma wasps:** Harmless to humans, these insects actually are tiny wasps that attack moth eggs and butterfly larvae (caterpillars, that is). Release the wasps when temperatures are above 72°F (22°C).

To get the good insects to stick around, avoid indiscriminate use of broad-spectrum pesticides, which kill everything, good along with bad. If you do spray, use a type that specifically targets the pest you want to eliminate and that has minimal effect on beneficial insects.

Another way to encourage beneficial insects to make a home of your flower bed is to maintain a diverse garden with many kinds and sizes of plants. Diversity gives the beneficial insects places to hide and reproduce, and it also can provide an alternative food source for beneficial insects that eat pollen and flower nectar as well as other insects. Plants that attract beneficial insects include Queen Anne's lace, parsley (especially if you let the flower develop), sweet alyssum, dill, fennel, and yarrow.

Releasing beneficial insects is one example of biological control, but you can also use different kinds of bacteria that, although harmless to humans, make insect pests very sick and eventually very dead. The most common and useful bacteria are forms of Bacillus thuringiensis, or Bt, which kill the larvae of moths and butterflies — that is, caterpillars. One type of Bt (sold as milky spore) kills the larvae of Japanese beetles.

Botanical insecticides

Botanical insecticides are those that are made from plants. The following are most useful against the pests of annual flowers:

✔ **Neem:** Derived from the tropical tree Azadirachta indica, neem kills young feeding insects and deters adult insects, but is harmless to people and to most beneficial insects. Neem works slowly and is effective against aphids, thrips, whiteflies, and, to a lesser degree, Japanese beetles.

I prefer neem oil over neem extract (check the product label) because oil is also effective against two common diseases: powdery mildew and rust. Neem oil gets thick when cool, so you must warm it up before mixing it with water. Neem is most effective when applied early in the morning or late in the evening when humidity is high. Reapply after rain.

✔ **Pyrethrin:** Derived from the painted daisy, Chrysanthemum cinerariifolium, pyrethrin is a broad-spectrum insecticide, meaning that it kills a wide range of insects, both good and bad. The nondiscriminatory nature of pyrethrin is the downside. The upside is that this insecticide kills pests such as thrips and beetles quickly and has low toxicity to mammals, making it essentially harmless to humans and the environment. (Spray late in the evening to avoid killing bees.)

The terminology can be confusing, here. Pyrethrum is the ground-up flower of the daisy. Pyrethrin is the insecticidal component of the flower. Pyrethroids, such as permethrin and resmethrin, are synthetic compounds that resemble pyrethrins but are more toxic and persistent. Consequently, I prefer to avoid pyrethroids for home garden use.

✔ **Rotenone:** Derived from the roots of tropical legumes, rotenone breaks down quickly but is more toxic than some commonly used traditional insecticides. It is a broad-spectrum insecticide, killing beneficial insects, including bees and pests alike. Use it as a last resort to control various caterpillars, beetles, and thrips.

Summer oil

When sprayed on a plant, this highly refined oil smothers insect pests and their eggs. The words highly refined, in this case, mean that the sulfur and other components of the oil that damage the plant are removed. It is relatively nontoxic and short-lived. Use it to control aphids, mites, thrips, and certain caterpillars.

Double-check the product label to make sure that the oil can be used on annual flowers during the growing season. Then follow the mixing instructions carefully. Water the plants before and after applying summer oil, and don't spray if temperatures are likely to rise above 85°F (29°C). When it's that hot, the oil can damage plant leaves.

Insecticidal soaps

Derived from the salts of fatty acids, insecticidal soaps kill mostly soft-bodied pests such as aphids, spider mites, and whiteflies. They also can be effective against Japanese beetles. Insecticidal soaps work fast, break down quickly, and are nontoxic to humans. They are most effective when mixed with soft water. Soaps sometimes burn tender foliage.

Synthetic insecticides

You can successfully control most insect problems by using the techniques and products described in the previous sections. If, however, a pest really gets out of hand on a prized planting, you may want to use something more serious. In the descriptions of insect pests, two synthetic pesticides are listed as possible solutions for a few pests: carbaryl (sold as Sevin) and acephate (usually sold as Orthene). Try other control measures before you resort to these products — using them will likely disrupt the balance of your garden. When you use any pesticide, make sure that you have the pest identified correctly and follow label instructions precisely.

Disease — When the Flower Bed Becomes a Sick Bed

Only a few diseases are really troublesome for annual flowers, and you can prevent or at least reduce in severity most of them by observing good cultural practices or by planting resistant varieties. If you know that a certain disease is a problem on a particular annual in your area, simply plant something else. You surely have many other choices, and you probably will broaden your gardening enjoyment by looking for other flowers.

Prevention and control

Here are some cultural practices that can help prevent plant diseases:

- ✔ **Remove infected plants.** After you notice a plant with a problem, give it the yank.

- ✔ **Avoid overhead watering.** Or at least water early in the morning so that plants have a chance to dry off before nightfall. Drip irrigation or watering in furrows, as I describe in Chapter 8, also helps keep foliage dry.

- ✔ **Space plants properly.** Planting annuals too close together reduces air circulation between plants, creating conditions that favor disease.

- ✔ **Prepare the soil.** Add organic matter to increase drainage and aeration, as I describe in Chapter 6. Doing so helps you sidestep many soilborne diseases.

- ✔ **Keep your garden clean and tidy.** Many diseases spread on plant debris, so rake up fallen leaves and remove dead plants. Simply removing diseased leaves can slow the spread of some organisms.

- ✔ **Rotate plants.** Don't put the same annuals in the same beds year after year. Doing so creates a breeding ground for disease. Plant something new.

Chemical fungicides are among the nastiest pesticides. They can contain some very toxic compounds that linger in the environment for a long time. If you can, try not to use them. If, however, a prized planting comes up with a really stubborn disease, you may feel that you have no other choice. Before you spray, make sure to identify the disease properly. Enlist the help of a local nursery or cooperative extension specialist. Then use a product specifically labeled for that disease occurring on the plants that you are growing. Follow the label instructions exactly.

Five feisty diseases

Here are some tips on how to prevent, identify, and — if possible — treat some common diseases of annual flowers:

✔ **Botrytis blight:** Also called gray mold, this fungal disease overwinters (survives in the soil or on plant debris through the winter to reinfect the plant again in spring) on plant debris and is common on petunias and ageratum, among others. It's most notable as gray fuzz forming on old flowers, turning them to moldy mush (see Figure 12-9), but it can also discolor or spot foliage. Botrytis blight is most troublesome on older plant parts and in cool, humid weather. To discourage this disease, make sure that plants are properly spaced and avoid overhead watering. Remove and destroy any infected plant parts and give your garden a good cleaning at the end of each growing season.

Figure 12-9: Botrytis blight can turn flowers to moldy mush.

✔ **Damping off:** This fungus attacks the base of seedling stems, causing them to wilt and fall over. (See Figure 12-10.) The best way to prevent the disease is to plant seeds in sterile potting soil and avoid overwatering. After the disease gets a foothold, it's hard to stop.

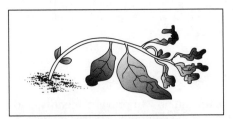

Figure 12-10: Damping off can be hard to control.

✔ **Powdery mildew:** This fungus coats leaves and flowers
with a white powder. (See Figure 12-11.) It is most common
when days are warm but nights are cool, and it is particularly troublesome on zinnias, dahlias, begonias, and
cosmos. Control is difficult, but resistant varieties of
those flowers are available. The disease also becomes
less of a problem as the weather changes, so if you keep
young plants growing vigorously, they may grow out of it.
Neem oil also may help. Near the end of the growing
season, you may want to pull out the diseased plants
early and start with something new next year.

Figure 12-11: Powdery mildew thrives during warm days and cool nights.

✔ **Rust:** This fungal disease is easy to identify: It forms
rusty pustules on the undersides of plant leaves. (See
Figure 12-12.) Gradually, the upper sides of the leaves
turn yellow, and the whole plant begins to decline.
Snapdragons and hollyhocks are common hosts.

To avoid rust, plant resistant varieties. Also, space plants
to allow good air circulation, keep the garden clean, and
avoid overhead watering. Destroy infected plants.

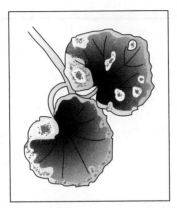

Figure 12-12: Rust is an easy fungus to identify.

✔ **Root rot:** Several soilborne fungi cause plants to basically do the same thing — suddenly wilt and die (see Figure 12-13); regardless of whether the soil is moist. Vinca is notorious for checking out like this. The best way to prevent root rot is to prepare the soil properly before planting and make sure that you aren't overwatering — let the soil dry partially in between irrigations. Otherwise, all you can do is remove the dead plants. Few other control measures are effective.

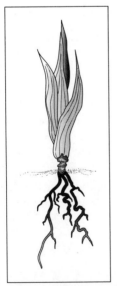

Figure 12-13: Root rot may be caused by overwatering.

Chapter 13

Ten Most Frequently Asked Questions about Annuals

● ●

*I*n the plant kingdom, annuals may be considered fun-
loving goof-offs, great to have around for a good time in the
summer — and even longer than that in mild climates. But
gardeners still have a fair share of questions about these care-
free, easy-to-grow flowers.

What is an annual?

Here's the short answer: An annual is a plant that goes
through its whole life cycle, from seed to bloom to creation of
new seeds, in one growing season. Unlike perennials, annuals
do not return year after year — although, if you're lucky, the
seeds they produce will germinate to take their places. Check
out Chapter 1 for more about what makes an annual an annual.

Should I plant seeds or seedlings?

The answer depends on the type of annual you want to grow.
Some annuals do best when they're sown directly in the
ground. Sunflowers and zinnias, for example, don't relish
transplanting. Sow seeds of those flowers right where you
want them to grow.

Other annuals do well whether you grow them directly from seeds sown in the ground or from seedlings. For example, marigolds grow no matter which way you start them.

You can start many annuals from seeds indoors and transplant them to the garden at the right time. This method saves money, if you want big quantities of certain plants. It can also be a rewarding aspect of gardening. But you may not want to start difficult, slow-growing types of annuals, such as impatiens or petunias, from seeds. You have better luck if you start slower-growing flowers like these from nursery-grown seedlings.

Is it better to plant big seedlings or little ones?

Nurseries usually offer annuals in a small six-pack size or in 4-inch pots or gallon cans. Annuals in larger containers usually are blooming and hard to resist. The blooming plants have one big advantage — they can brighten a garden instantly. But the smaller plants can generally outperform the bigger ones. In fact, if the little seedlings have flowers on them, cut off the blooms when you plant them to encourage bushier growth and more flower production in the long run.

When can I plant annuals?

The answer depends on where you live. If you live in a typical cold-winter climate, plant tender annuals (the ones that frost will kill) after all danger of frost has passed. You can plant hardy annuals a few weeks earlier. Some annuals (such as zinnias) need warm soil and air temperatures as well as no threat of frost; plant these flowers when the weather really starts to heat up.

If you live in milder climates, the planting schedule can get a little more complicated (in a good way). For example, you may be able to plant in the fall for winter and spring bloom. See Chapters 3 and 4 for a gardening calendar appropriate for your season.

As a general rule, don't plant the instant that nurseries start selling annuals.

Why do I see the same plants at every nursery?

Nurseries sell flowers that are the most popular. (After all, they're in it for the money.) Petunias, impatiens, and marigolds are very popular plants because they're reliable, easy to grow, and long-blooming. But hundreds of other wonderful varieties are available. To discover other varieties, check out mail-order catalogs and specialty nurseries.

What's eating my annuals?

Most annuals are relatively trouble-free, but they can sometimes run into problems with pests or diseases. (See Chapter 12.) The problem may be that you're growing a plant that's not suited for your climate or garden. With so many terrific annuals, why not choose something else? That's my garden philosophy. Where I live, budworms always eat petunias, and my zinnias always get mildew, so I grow something else. If your nasturtiums are what's getting eaten, the culprit may be your neighbor — nasturtiums make delicious salads!

What's the easiest-to-grow, most colorful annual?

Impatiens. Next question. . . .

What annuals can I get to bloom in the shade?

Impatiens can do wonders in deep shade, but they can also tolerate a lot of sun in cool climates. Bedding begonias, primroses, coleus, and spider flower also like shady spots. But even these shade-loving plants need some light to bloom well. If your shady spots are too dark, better try ferns.

Should I always cut off dead flowers?

This process is called deadheading, and it benefits most annuals by forcing them to concentrate on new flower production rather than seed production. Deadheading is easy with bigger flowers and is essential with zinnias, large-flowered marigolds, and many others. Small-flowered annuals (such as felicias) can sometimes be sheared. Some annuals, such as impatiens, are those miracles of the plant-breeders' art that are considered to be self-cleaning — no deadheading required.

What annuals can I grow to attract butterflies?

To get butterflies to linger in your garden, you must provide nectar plants for the adult butterflies and tasty foliage for the caterpillars to chew on. Annuals can't do the whole butterfly-attracting job by themselves, but they can make butterflies happy and add beauty to your garden. Try phlox, verbena, zinnia, and Mexican sunflower (Tithonia).

Index

SPORTS, FITNESS, PARENTING, RELIGION & SPIRITUALITY

0-471-76871-5

0-7645-7841-3

Also available:

- Catholicism For Dummies
  0-7645-5391-7
- Exercise Balls For Dummies
  0-7645-5623-1
- Fitness For Dummies
  0-7645-7851-0
- Football For Dummies
  0-7645-3936-1
- Judaism For Dummies
  0-7645-5299-6
- Potty Training For Dummies
  0-7645-5417-4
- Buddhism For Dummies
  0-7645-5359-3

- Pregnancy For Dummies
  0-7645-4483-7 †
- Ten Minute Tone-Ups
  For Dummies
  0-7645-7207-5
- NASCAR For Dummies
  0-7645-7681-X
- Religion For Dummies
  0-7645-5264-3
- Soccer For Dummies
  0-7645-5229-5
- Women in the Bible
  For Dummies
  0-7645-8475-8

TRAVEL

0-7645-7749-2

0-7645-6945-7

Also available:

- Alaska For Dummies
  0-7645-7746-8
- Cruise Vacations For Dummies
  0-7645-6941-4
- England For Dummies
  0-7645-4276-1
- Europe For Dummies
  0-7645-7529-5
- Germany For Dummies
  0-7645-7823-5
- Hawaii For Dummies
  0-7645-7402-7

- Italy For Dummies
  0-7645-7386-1
- Las Vegas For Dummies
  0-7645-7382-9
- London For Dummies
  0-7645-4277-X
- Paris For Dummies
  0-7645-7630-5
- RV Vacations For Dummies
  0-7645-4442-X
- Walt Disney World & Orlando
  For Dummies
  0-7645-9660-8

GRAPHICS, DESIGN & WEB DEVELOPMENT

0-7645-8815-X

0-7645-9571-7

Also available:

- 3D Game Animation For
  Dummies
  0-7645-8789-7
- AutoCAD 2006 For Dummies
  0-7645-8925-3
- Building a Web Site For
  Dummies
  0-7645-7144-3
- Creating Web Pages All-in-
  One Desk Reference For
  Dummies
  0-7645-4345-8
- Dreamweaver 8 For Dummies
  0-7645-9649-7
- InDesign CS2 For Dummies
  0-7645-9572-5

- Macromedia Flash 8
  For Dummies
  0-7645-9691-8
- Photoshop CS2 and Digital
  Photography For Dummies
  0-7645-9580-6
- Photoshop Elements 4
  For Dummies
  0-471-77483-9
- Syndicating Web Sites with
  RSS Feeds For Dummies
  0-7645-8848-6
- Yahoo! SiteBuilder
  For Dummies
  0-7645-9800-7

NETWORKING, SECURITY, PROGRAMMING & DATABASES

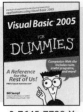

0-7645-7728-X

0-471-74940-0

Also available:

- Access 2003 All-in-One Desk
  Reference For Dummies
  0-7645-3988-4
- ASP.NET 2 For Dummies
  0-7645-7907-X
- C# 2005 For Dummies
  0-7645-9704-3
- Excel VBA Programming
  For Dummies
  0-7645-7412-4
- Hacking For Dummies
  0-7645-5784-X
- Hacking Wireless Networks
  For Dummies
  0-7645-9730-2

- Microsoft SQL Server 2005
  For Dummies
  0-7645-7755-7
- Networking All-in-One Desk
  Reference For Dummies
  0-7645-9939-9
- Preventing Identity Theft
  For Dummies
  0-7645-7336-5
- Telecom For Dummies
  0-471-77085-X
- Visual Studio 2005 All-in-One
  Desk Reference For Dummies
  0-7645-9775-2
- XML For Dummies
  0-7645-8845-1

HEALTH & SELF-HELP

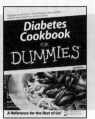 

0-7645-8450-2   0-7645-4149-8

Also available:

- Bipolar Disorder For Dummies
  0-7645-8451-0
- Chemotherapy and
  Radiation
  For Dummies
  0-7645-7832-4
- Controlling Cholesterol
  For Dummies
  0-7645-5440-9
- Diabetes For Dummies
  0-7645-6820-5* †
- Divorce For Dummies
  0-7645-8417-0 †
- Fibromyalgia For Dummies
  0-7645-5441-7

- Low-Calorie Dieting
  For Dummies
  0-7645-9905-4
- Meditation For Dummies
  0-471-77774-9
- Osteoporosis For Dummies
  0-7645-7621-6
- Overcoming Anxiety
  For Dummies
  0-7645-5447-6
- Reiki For Dummies
  0-7645-9907-0
- Stress Management
  For Dummies
  0-7645-5144-2

EDUCATION, HISTORY, REFERENCE & TEST PREPARATION

0-7645-8381-6   0-7645-9554-7

Also available:

- The ACT For Dummies
  0-7645-9652-7
- Algebra For Dummies
  0-7645-5325-9
- Algebra Workbook
  For Dummies
  0-7645-8467-7
- Astronomy For Dummies
  0-7645-8465-0
- Calculus For Dummies
  0-7645-2498-4
- Chemistry For Dummies
  0-7645-5430-1
- Forensics For Dummies
  0-7645-5580-4

- Freemasons For Dummies
  0-7645-9796-5
- French For Dummies
  0-7645-5193-0
- Geometry For Dummies
  0-7645-5324-0
- Organic Chemistry I
  For Dummies
  0-7645-6902-3
- The SAT I For Dummies
  0-7645-7193-1
- Spanish For Dummies
  0-7645-5194-9
- Statistics For Dummies
  0-7645-5423-9

Get smart @ dummies.com®

- **Find a full list of Dummies titles**
- **Look into loads of FREE on-site articles**
- **Sign up for FREE eTips e-mailed to you weekly**
- **See what other products carry the Dummies name**
- **Shop directly from the Dummies bookstore**
- **Enter to win new prizes every month!**

* Separate Canadian edition also available
† Separate U.K. edition also available

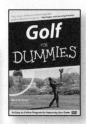

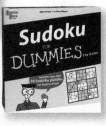

Portable Gardening Guides

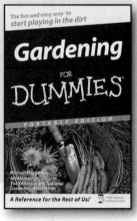

**Each book includes
8 pages of full-color
garden photos!**

Notes